A Pilgrim for Freedom

A Pilgrim for Freedom

ISBN 978-0-9979938-0-6

*I dedicate this book
to my wife, Phebe*

ଵୄଵ

Contents

Part Three: An Officer and a Gentleman

Part Four: From an Officer to a Businessman

Left to right: Phebe, Phebe Nevenka, Michael B. Novakovic, Jr. and Mike, Sr.

Above: The Novakovic grandchildren at The Philadelphia Club in August 2014; Top left: Son, Michael B. Novakovic, Jr. in Air Force Academy uniform — now an S.E.C. attorney, Philadelphia, PA; Bottom Left: Daughter, Phebe Nevenka Novakovic, college age — now CEO of General Dynamics

Acknowledgements

The original reason for writing this memoir is my close relationship with my children and grandchildren. During the many family holidays, visits and vacations I have enjoyed with Alexandra, Natasha, Sophia, Michaela and Nikolas, I have shared episodes from my childhood in Croatia and then as a refugee in Italy during World War II. To capture these stories in one place, as well as to pass on one part of the Novakovic family history, I have assembled the following memories of growing up in Europe, South America, coming to the United States, serving in the U.S. military, starting a family and running a business. I thank Darryl Hart, an historian to whom I told my story, who helped me weave the events in my life into a whole, and who prodded me to reflect on the meaning of what were sometimes painful memories. This book could not have been written without him. Graham Humes, a great friend from our days in Philadelphia, provided encouragement and invaluable comments on the manuscript at different stages.

Writing about my life, however, was not nearly as hard as holding on to it. Here I need to give thanks to the U.S. fighter pilot, who when flying a strafing mission over Ancona, Italy, and seeing a boy stand up to wave at him, determined to stop firing rounds at potentially hostile persons on the ground. If that pilot had not returned my naive friendliness, I would likely have not survived World War II. I am also forever thankful to Colonel William Holleran (the officer responsible for the R.O.T.C. Program at Syracuse University), and the unnamed Sergeant who first introduced me to Colonel Holleran. He opened the door of military service to me, at the time a recent immigrant to the United States who still lacked citizenship, an introduction that would fulfill my dreams and set the course for my life. I joined the U.S. Air Force and established a memorable track record in Intelligence. (Colonel Holleran retired from the Air Force and became a senior civilian with the National Security Agency.) General H.P. Smith took notice of my work by making me his special operational assistant. He deserves recognition and thanks for the model military officer that he was and for taking me under his wing.

Beyond surviving war and serving in the greatest nation's armed services, my life would have been incomplete without my lovely and devoted wife of almost sixty years and our two wonderful children. I dedicate this book to my wife, Phebe. Anyone who reads the following pages can understand what a steady and loving companion Phebe has been to me, sacrificing so much. If not for her modesty, I would have included her more in this book. Sometimes less really is more, but my life would have been impoverished without all Phebe did to welcome, encourage and support a refugee from war-torn Europe who wanted to fight evil communism by joining the U.S. Armed Forces.

Villanova, Pennsylvania
August 2014

Foreword
by James Humes, Scholar

Our two World Wars traced their beginnings to Eastern Europe. The first World War was triggered by the assassination of an Archduke of Austria. The second World War was ignited by Nazis staging a shooting of a German at the Polish border.

Yet compared to Italy and Russia, central Europe from Budapest south to the Balkans, little is known to Americans. Eastern Europe is a welter of ethnic nationalities each competing for their own political identity and religion. Croatians identify with Rome and Catholicism; to the west, Serbs assert their Eastern Orthodox heritage and look eastward. Both rebel against the Muslim sect which was taking orders from Istanbul.

Three alphabets compete: Roman, Cyrillic and Turkish — not to mention the languages of the German, Italian and Russian occupiers of these eastern European territories.

Michael Novakovic, in his personal account of his family's pilgrimage to America, brings light to this conflicted area in a way professional historians have not. It is not an account of the maneuverings of prime ministers, presidents, diplomats and generals, but the gripping account of one family's trials and travels from what was then Yugoslavia to Trieste, Italy, to Argentina and finally the ultimate objective of their odyssey: The United States of America.

We know of the writings of Count de Toqueville to Lord Bryce that some of the most insightful analysis of American democracy came from foreign observers. Similarly, the most keen observations of America and its politics are often from outsiders. The majority of newly arrived visitors are often the most fervent converts to the American dream. The native-born American usually takes the freedom and opportunities America offers for granted. Not so the immigrant who contrasts it to his birth country.

(Lt.) Colonel Novakovic is not blind to the flaws of American society — the slums of the city, the prejudice against race, religion or an unfamiliar accent. He himself has occasionally experienced some of them. But he is also aware of the long waiting lists of immigrants for visas of passage to New York. He remembers that, before the Iron Curtain collapsed in 1989, there were no West Germans trying to climb the wall to escape to East Berlin. There were no lines of Austrians hoping to find asylum in neighboring then Communist Czechoslovakia. Or across the ocean, how many South Koreans were not trying to immigrate to North Korea. America, as Lincoln proclaimed, is "the last best hope of the world." The Statue of Liberty's torch is still the beacon of the world for the oppressed and the downtrodden.

The Novakovic family's trek to America is not unique. It replicates the accounts of millions before them. If Michael Novakovic can assert his claim to a Yugoslav dukedom now that his right of descent has been recognized, he did suffer the privations of the dispossessed like so many of the immigrants to our shores.

No Mayflower descendant, no Son of the American Revolution and no descendant of a Founding Father is prouder of his American heritage than Michael Novakovic. If he still speaks with an accent, so did the ancestors of virtually all Americans when they first arrived on our shores.

Michael Novakovic does not have to prove his patriotism. It is manifest by his pilgrimage to America, his service to his adopted beloved country, the life threatening risks he took, and the numerous medals he earned — including the Bronze Star Medal and the South Vietnamese Medal of Honor while in its service and his own fulfillment of the American dream — a source of inspiration for all future immigrants.

James Humes is a former White House speechwriter who drafted texts for four Chief Executives. A one-time Woodrow Wilson Scholar at the Smithsonian, he has authored over 35 books on Presidents and numerous speeches and is an authority on Winston Churchill.

Prologue

When I awoke on July 12th, 1943, the toothache I had been experiencing for over a week had become almost unbearable. I was eleven years old. We were a long way from our comfortable home in Split, Yugoslavia where we had experienced all the conveniences and comforts one could wish for. A visit to the dentist's office there would have been routine. Instead, here we were in a small village named Maggio in the mountains of northern Italy. There were perhaps 60 homes, one church, and one small pension. We were there because we were forced to flee Split when the Axis Powers made life impossible for us. In Split, people were disappearing, street executions were common occurrences — even I had been shot at on my way home from school. For over a year now we had suffered from lack of the barest of necessities of life including food and clothing. A toothbrush did not exist.

I went to my parents stating that my toothache was much worse and asked what I was to do. They responded that my brother Paul and I should borrow bicycles and ride down the mountain to Viggiu, a small town at the foot of the mountain. There, they said, we would find a dentist. Paul and I had no difficulty locating bikes for the journey. After all, biking was the major form of public transportation.

The ride into Viggiu would be easy — it was all down hill. The five miles would probably take some 10 minutes. Of course, coming back we knew would be a struggle — a ninety minute uphill strenuous ride. As it turned out, the ride to Maggio would make the return trip seem effortless.

Paul and I hopped on the borrowed bikes and headed down the mountainside. Suddenly we heard gun shots and numerous explosions coming from the direction we were heading. We were, by that time, out of sight of Maggio. At first we were undecided whether to proceed or to return to the village. But this was wartime and we had grown accustomed to explosions, gunfire, and bombings. After all, we had first heard these sounds in our homeland of Yugoslavia and we had now been in Italy for over a year. Gunshots, no matter how close, were neither a surprise nor a reason to abandon our mission. How wrong we were!

We turned a corner on that winding, dirt road leading to Viggiu and saw a horrific scene. A woman was lying in the middle of the road, pleading for mercy from a group of men who were attacking her. Communist Partisans were stabbing her with bayonets and torturing her. They seemed determined to inflict as much pain as possible on her and other victims and to prolong the agony as long as possible before killing them. Around the woman, strewn on the sides of the road, were dying Italian body guards who had been assigned as protection for the woman. The Partisans had shot some of them. Others were being savagely wounded and then killed with bayonets — some directly into their faces. The trucks and automobile that had carried these victims were smoldering, and the doors on the automobile carrying the woman were swinging from their hinges. However, the damages to the vehicles could not compare to the awful condition of the humans on the ground. Blood was flowing everywhere. It was a ghastly sight. The guards, who had survived the initial attack, were being eviscerated before finally being bayoneted. One guard tried to escape but was recaptured and returned to the leader who ordered the guard's arms and feet bound. Then a steel rod with a hook at one end, was inserted into his mouth and he was impelled to a hanging position — a favorite Communist execution. Screams echoed throughout the valley.

It was only the chaos that allowed my brother and me to escape and head on down the road. It was a scene I would not experience again during the rest of World War II or serving as a soldier in the Vietnam War. It was right out of Dante's Inferno. What made this attack even more frightening for me was that I knew the woman. She was the wife of an Italian Senior Officer who was a member of Benito Mussolini's inner circle. Her daughter was one of our village playmates.

As awful as that was, I also needed to give attention to our own safety, not to mention my toothache about which I had entirely forgotten. Shock can be an amazing pain killer. We did eventually find the dentist; but as soon as I sat in the chair, we heard explosions and gunfire in the town so we had to flee the dentist's office and Paul and I once again were on our bikes — this time going up the dirt road to Maggio. This route took us by the nightmarish scene once more, but by then the Communist Partisans had faded back into the mountains. Bodies were still strewn across the landscape. The woman now lay with a large boulder placed across her head. The Partisans had sufficient strength and know how to massacre even well protected family members of Italy's Fascist government. As Paul and I rode on to the village, not a word was spoken. The war was forcing us to grow up very fast.

We didn't talk much about what we had seen. We had witnessed the horrors of war — from the incessant struggles between European ideologues to the global conflict that kept our family hemmed in within Italy — unable to find a safe refuge, uncertain about the place we would call home after the fighting. But we had never experienced anything as inhumane as those tortures. It was, of course, an important lesson on the tolls that war could take on humans and the hatred that fueled European political ideologies of both Fascism and Communism. It was a testament to Communist barbarism and Axis and Nazi insanity.

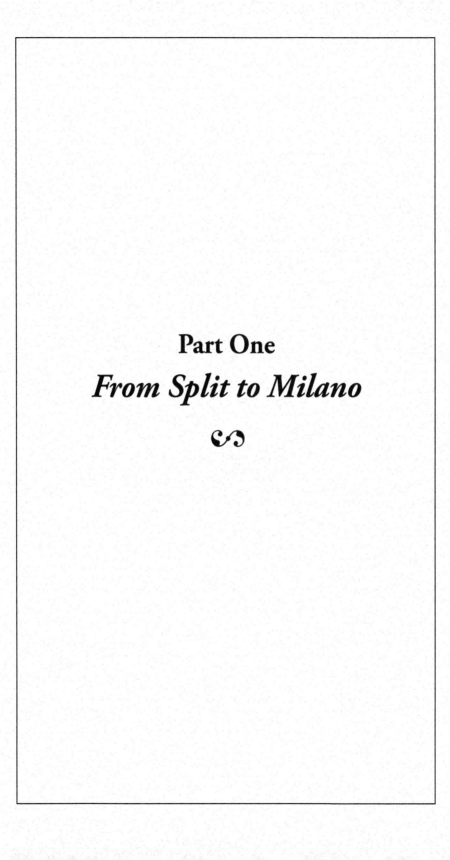

Part One
From Split to Milano

∾

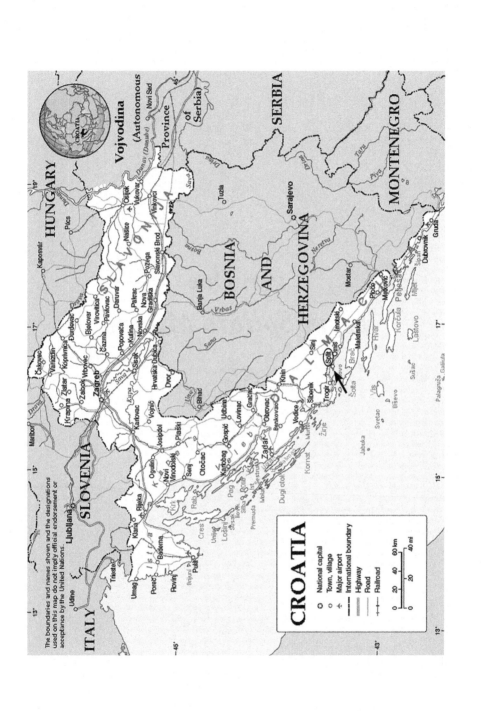

The boundaries and names shown and the designations used on this map do not imply official endorsement or acceptance by the United Nations.

CROATIA

○ National capital
○ Town, village
✈ Major airport
--- International boundary
— Highway
— Road
++++ Railroad

0   20   40   60 km
0   20   40 mi

CHAPTER 1

Going on "A Picnic"

About 18 months before my toothache, on a warm spring day in April 1942, I walked with my mother and three siblings, Deana, Gordana, and Paul, down to the docks in Split, Croatia, to board a boat headed for Pula, a town on the Istrian peninsula along the northeastern coast of the Adriatic Sea. It was a voyage on a ship that took one-and-a-half days (about 500 kilometers by car) and carried approximately fifty passengers. This was not your average recreational excursion. The expansion of Italy and Germany into the former Yugoslavia was adding to the strife and armed conflict that beset my home-town the better part of a decade. But we told all our friends and neighbors, as well as the agents selling tickets, that we were taking a three day trip to Italy.

It was the last time I would see Split until 2005 when my wife, Phebe, and I returned and saw the consequences of another war among the peoples who had united under the name, Yugoslavia, or "Land of the South Slavs." We were leaving behind a world we would never experience again, thank God. The governess would not be getting us up and dressed. There would be no formal breakfast in the dining room. We would no longer have our morning walks by the sea. There would be no more Sunday dinners with our grandparents with large gold coins placed under our plates, which would not be available until after we had eaten everything on those plates. Trips carrying food to the needy from our grandmother's kitchen would stop. Warm afternoons on the beaches, swimming in the blue Adriatic Sea would only be memories. Playing in the old city squares and exploring the catacombs of Diocletian's palace was over. We would never again spend our summers in Lake Bled, Lubljana or in our cottage on Marjan Mountain overlooking the Adriatic. The unofficial school uniform consisting of a white shirt and blue short pants would disappear from my wardrobe. (I wasn't too sad about that since I didn't like the rounded collar on the shirt. I thought it was girlish.) My father's car collection, which included one Mercedes with a rumble seat that we all fought to ride in, was left behind. Picasso paintings and other paintings on the walls of the parlor had to be left in place. All of this became a previous life.

Armed conflict had afflicted this part of Europe for much of the twentieth century prior to my birth on May 31, 1932. But by 1942, when my family left Split that spring day, Italy's invasion of Yugoslavia on April 6, 1941, had transformed the perennial tensions among the Croatians, Serbs, and Muslims in the Balkans into a full-blown international conflict — one sector among many in the initial phases of World War II. The war nipped at our heels on our voyage up the Adriatic Sea. The ship's captain told us to move to the side of the boat nearest land lest torpedoes aimed by British submarines from the sea side inflict heavy casualties on passengers while sinking the boat. One of the ships making this route had already been sunk the previous week by a British submarine.

We packed only enough to fill one bag and left everything else behind — including my father. This was to allay suspicions of our intentions. This was supposed to be a brief trip, allegedly for the purpose of sightseeing and relaxation. We did take with us one essential — money, more specifically, gold coins. The war and the economy made most local currencies incredibly unreliable and potentially worthless. My mother and father actually had each one of the children wrap gold coins to our bodies, under our clothes. We even hid gold in the few toys we were able to take. Obviously, this was no vacation.

We needed those coins right away once we arrived at our true destination, Trieste, Italy. Pula was merely a ruse to get as close to a new location where we hoped to blend in and escape the danger that afflicted Serbians in my hometown of Split. Gold bought my family's papers of transit that permitted us to find a relatively safe harbor in Italy as Italian citizens. Language was not a problem since we had native fluency in Italian. In the Dalmatian province of Croatia, our lives were in danger, and my father had already been imprisoned by Fascist soldiers when the Axis powers began to control the former Yugoslavia. And just as my mother was able to buy my father's freedom by bribing Italian officers, so we could buy Italian citizenship and with it time to figure out where we would go next — not for fame, fortune, or success, but simply to stay alive. Like the people who passed through Rick's Café in the movie *Casablanca*, in Trieste we could purchase almost anything. And what our family wanted more than anything was to escape the war in Croatia where we had little chance for survival.

Over the next decade my nationality would change four times, whether the various national officials knew it or not. It started with Yugoslavia.

The first Yugoslavia emerged out of the ashes of World War I, created through the merger of the mostly Roman Catholic regions of Slovenia and Croatia with the Eastern Orthodox Kingdoms of Serbia and Montenegro. Included in the new nation was the land of Bosnia, ethnically and religiously divided among Roman Catholic Croats, Orthodox Serbs and a small minority of Muslim Slavs. In southern Yugoslavia lay the region of Kosovo, the hallowed ground of the Serbs which since 1975 has been dominated by an Albanian population that is now mostly Muslim.

This land of many nationalities began — the first Yugoslavia — on December 1, 1918 when Croatia, a state that had recently declared independence, united with the Kingdom of Serbia, to form the Kingdom of Yugoslavia. Various Croatian groups were never happy with this arrangement and feared a state dominated by the Serbs. Not surprisingly, the Croats were opposed. In 1921 Yugoslavia adopted a constitution with a parliamentary form of government and Alexander, the king of Serbia, was recognized as the constitutional monarch of Yugoslavia. But opposition from the Croats and the senseless assassination of a Croat leader prompted Alexander in 1929 to abolish the constitution and establish a regime under his rule. Unfortunately, this was the kind of rivalry and treachery that had characterized the region for the better part of four centuries.

Two years later the king instituted a new constitution that was designed to expand his power. But opposition to his reign persisted and on October 9, 1934 an assassin killed the king during a trip to Marseilles where Alexander was seeking to strengthen ties with France. It was the first assassination recorded on film. The assassin, from Bulgaria, was part of an organization that sought independence for Macedonia from Yugoslavia. The conditions in Yugoslavia during Alexander's dictatorship prompted Albert Einstein to write that a "horrible brutality" was "being practiced upon the Croatian People."

Obviously, not all Croats opposed the Serbs since my parents represented each side of that historic antagonism. My father was a Serb who had grown up in Knin, Croatia and my mother was a Croatian from the city of Split. Personal affection like the one between my parents was not totally uncommon in Yugoslavia. What was customary was a deep ethnic loyalty to political self-determination and to the rulers, leaders, parties, and armies who represented the nationalist hopes of Croatians, Serbs, Slovenians, and Muslims.

The struggles among the Slavs obviously were not the only sources of antagonism in Europe during my childhood. I remember one night we were sitting in our very spacious and well appointed living room listening to the radio. That night on September 1, 1939, when I was eight years old, we heard the news reports of Germany's invasion of Poland. My parents did not talk to us about politics and the possibility of war.

But all of us sensed that the strife and unrest we were experiencing periodically in Split and throughout our region were being swallowed up in an international conflict. We also sensed what our parents already knew — we could not stay in Split for long.

Until 1939, Yugoslavia continued under the rule of Alexander's son, Prince Peter II, then a minor who was dependent on a regent council to guide the affairs of state. Fears of an expansionist Germany exploiting Croatian discontent in 1939 led the government to grant Croatia the separate status of a banovina (from the Slavic word for province or region under the rule of a "ban" or lord). But the tensions between Croats and Serbs could not withstand the April 6, 1941 invasion of the Axis powers (Germany, Italy, and Bulgaria). While Germany acquired much of the former Yugoslavia, the historic province of Dalmatia, where both of my parents and I were born and had grown up, went to the Italians who had already been flexing their muscles along the eastern coast of the Adriatic Sea.

The Axis occupation of my parents' homeland was a major blow to my parents' hopes for carrying on their life in Split. My father and mother already well understood that not only their livelihoods but their lives were in danger. For that reason we determined to go on a "picnic" to Italy. It turned out to be a trip without a return ticket and the first stage of a much longer voyage that would take me to South America, the United States, and even to Asia, and to the North Pole.

CHAPTER 2

Banker's Holiday

I f I had been born in the United States, my birthday, May 31, 1932, would have almost coincided with the national observance of Memorial Day. (I was born on a Tuesday and Memorial Day is typically on Monday.) The American holiday first emerged as a way for African-Americans in the South to honor the Union soldiers who had died in the Civil War. By the 1870s most states designated a day in May to honor all soldiers who had died in that conflict. By the era in which I was born it became a day to honor all American soldiers who had died in battle (though it would not become a national holiday until an act of Congress in 1967). But since I was born in Croatia, May 31 was not a holiday in the Kingdom of Yugoslavia.

As it turned out, at least in the city of Split where my father, Branko Novakovic, was the director of the Serbian National Bank, it became

Mike (left) with father and Paul, 1940

one. Since he was functionally the president of this bank, he had the power to open and close its doors at his discretion. On the day of my birth, my father decided to close the bank's operations and celebrate the birth of his first son, who was also the first descendent from my

6

father's side of the family to carry on the Novakovic name. Obviously, this practice of closing businesses with the birth of a son does not exist in the United States. My sisters, Gordana and Deana, both older than I, always ribbed me about receiving special treatment from my father, which was an indication of prerogatives that men enjoyed in the Old World.

My father's birthplace of Knin is a small town near the headwaters of the Krka River, a mid point between Split and Zagreb. Knin has always been relatively small compared to the bigger cities in Croatia and Serbia, but at two points in its storied past this town occupied a prominent place in both the history of the Croatians and the Serbs. In the eleventh century, when it was the capital of the Kingdom of Croatia, the town had a sign which bore the message, "Welcome to Knin, town of King Dmitar Zvonimir." This kingdom lasted for only three centuries, but Knin's strategic geographic position and military

Branko Novakovic, Mike's father in WWI uniform

fortress played an important role in many wars and changes in power in the region, which included the Kingdom of Hungary, the Venetians, the Turks, the Austrians and the French. In 1522, the Ottoman Empire took control of Knin and the town became a Serbian stronghold because of Turkish policies that encouraged Serbian refugees to take the place of Croatians who had fled to escape Ottoman rule. The fort in Knin became the base for Austro-Hungarian resistance to the Muslims, an endeavor in which Serbs and Croats together fought, despite their religious differences. No matter how small Knin remained, its history and significance would always be bound up with Europe's defeat of the Ottomans' designs upon Christendom.

Knin's significance to the Serbs was also responsible for the town's second period of prominence. In 1991, after the breakup of Yugoslavia under the Communist rule and the declaration of Croatian independence, Knin became the capital of the Republic of Serbian Krajina. Although never recognized internationally, this Serbian Republic was the outlet for Serbian separatist movements during the Balkan conflict.

Because of the historic presence of Serbs in Knin, my father's family had lived there for at least four hundred years. I possess the will of my great grandfather from 1780 which specified his debts and instructed his sons to settle with his creditors. As priests, they were not wealthy, even if their service in Knin did merit a Novakovic Street, named in their honor. A small lake and waterfalls also bear the Novakovic name. My ancestors on my father's side had served in the Serbian Orthodox Church for generations. My paternal grandfather was also a priest, but he encouraged his sons to find work that was more lucrative. My father's chosen career was banking. He trained in Vienna, and one of his first jobs was at a bank in Zagreb. He remained on good terms with the man who had first hired him after he became director of the bank in Split. I remember accompanying my father to visit his former colleague in Zagreb. One of the lessons I learned during those trips was a piece of Old World wisdom about how to wash one's hands. The former colleague told me not to let the water run over the soap as I washed my hands. His logic was that to do so wasted water and soap. Whenever I visited him after that I did not like to wash my hands. As it turned out, this advice was good preparation for what awaited me when I turned nine. During the four years when my family and I were in Italy, trying to avoid the fighting of World War II, soap and clean water were luxuries. Still, even though I had few occasions to wash my hands (or the rest of my body for that matter) in Italy, that lesson about not wasting soap or water remained etched in my memory.

As I later came to understand in America, my father was a man who gained success and a privileged lifestyle by practicing the tenet of his family's religion, and living a life of honor and perseverance. He worked very hard, all day and most evenings at home, but he did enjoy the fruits of his labor. Although my mother's family was prominent in Split, my parents' wealth came almost exclusively from my father's work and responsibilities at the bank. While directing the bank in Split, my father met my mother and they were married in 1924. They lived very comfortably and could afford a cook, maid, chauffeur, and a variety of nannies (some of them not the most patient with children), who also functioned as governesses to me and my three siblings. I particularly disliked a German one who was a constant annoyance.

As comfortable as our home was in Split, the best indication of my father's success as a banker was his automobiles. At one point he owned three cars when simply owning one was a novelty — at the time, Split had approximately six automobiles in the entire city. In 1939, he bought a new maroon Mercury to accompany a green Mercedes coupe that he liked to drive for weekend

Mike's father and his Buick, 1939

excursions to the countryside where our villa was located. My dad was so proud of this new luxury car that he had a garage built within our regular garage to keep dust from building up on his prized Mercury. This was also the car that the chauffeur would use to take my father and the family to different functions and events. But for his daily work at the bank, my dad walked. This luxury car was simply that — a luxury. It was also a love that he passed on to me since, over the course of my life, I owned as many as seventy-five cars, from a dilapidated twelve-year-old Oldsmobile that drank oil almost as fast as it burned gas — my first that I bought as an undergraduate university student — to a Mercedes S-Class 600, my current car of choice.

When we left Split, both my parents made a great sacrifice. My father's first job after the war was carrying luggage as a bellhop in New York City. At the same time, my mother worked long and difficult hours as a seamstress in the garment district of New York. It is hard to calculate which of my parents gave up more. In the case of my father, he would never recover the prominence or wealth for which he had trained and worked so hard in Yugoslavia. But because of his success our family had the means to escape with our lives the terrors of war that on the day I was born seemed inconceivable to a man who closed a bank to celebrate the arrival of his first son with his wife and daughters.

Mike's Grandfather Theodore Novakovic,
a Serbian Orthodox Priest

CHAPTER 3

Seen But Not Heard

Before we left for Trieste in search of a safe haven during World War II, my experience with gold coins was infrequent. Yet, they were abundant during our trip as practically our only means of survival. Before the voyage, I held them only one at a time as part of a much hoped for gift when visiting my grandparents' home on Sundays for a formal dinner in their elegant dining room. As a boy, it was difficult sitting through all of the courses of food and behaving so as to be seen and not heard — which was the rule for all the children around the table. Now when I think about the value of the silver and crystal used in that dining room I understand. My favorite food was palacinkas, a Czech version of the crepe suzette, thin pancakes filled with cream and marmalade. We sometimes had them at the Sunday dinners. To add further interest for the children, my grandparents usually would place a gold ducat — usually an Austrian Krone — under our plates. It was thrilling to lift the plate, after eating everything on it, and retrieve a piece of gold. When the coin was there, I found Sunday dinner to be much more bearable than if I had to wait to be excused so I could play with my brother, Paul. Eventually, I lost all of those coins when the Fascist soldiers, who invaded Yugoslavia, came to our home and took the gold while rummaging through all of our family's possessions.

Those coins, like the ornate plates under which they were hidden and the elegant tablecloth on which they were placed, were one small indication of my mother's family's wealth and status. Her maiden name was Nevenka Juras and she had lived, like several generations before her, in Split, the second largest city in Croatia and the urban center of the Dalmatian province. The city has a long history that dates back to the original sixth-century B.C. Greek colony of the same name. The name itself comes from a plant that grows wildly in the area, the "spiny broom," which in Greek was *spalathos*. Under Greek influence, the city's name was Aspalathos. When the city came within the orbit of the Roman Empire, the Latinized word *spalatum* became the basis for referring to the city as Spatulum, eventually shortened to the modern name of Split.

Part of the city's fame, which also accrued to my mother's family, were sections of the palace built there in the early fourth century A.D. by the Roman Emperor Diocletian for his retirement. The palace was massive, and for all intents and purposes, a military fortress. Its walls measured 700 feet long and 70 feet high, and an area of more than nine acres was enclosed. This palace also functioned as a walled city and during the emperor's life sheltered as many as 9,000 inhabitants who served the emperor and supported themselves. After passing between Roman and Byzantine rule, by the seventh century the palace had become the city of Split and to this day remains the inner core of the city with shops, markets, and parks.

Remains of Diocletian Palace, Split.
Mike's grandparents owned part of the building.

My mother's family owned a part of that palace. In fact, they lived in part of the wall that faced the Adriatic Sea, the most desirable part of the palace. The wall was at least twenty-five feet wide, large enough to provide space for four apartments. Today my grandparents' home has been divided into separate units, but during my boyhood my mother's family lived on all four levels, with one level dedicated to bedrooms, another to a dining room and kitchen, and another to living rooms and visitors' and servants' quarters. Part of the catacombs were also included. Tito and the Communists would eventually take away all private property.

Mike's grandfather Juras, the owner of floors in the Diocletian Palace, Split

When the Communist government collapsed in 1991, however, the part of the palace that my family owned was partially returned to my mother's descendants. This meant that my oldest sister and I became the unlikely holders of the deed to a part of the Diocletian Palace. The most memorable part of the palace for me as a boy was not the residence of my grandparents but the catacombs in which my brother Paul and I played after we received permission to leave the dinner table. We would dare each other to see how far we could go into those dank and dark spaces. Without any light — not even a flashlight — it took some courage to venture very far before we turned around and fled back to the entrance. Eventually we graduated to candlesticks and human powered small battery lamps, a new invention from Germany.

In addition to owning part of the city's oldest structure, my mother's family also had great wealth from several business enterprises which included one of the first, and for a time, the only automobile manufacturer in Yugoslavia. My maternal grandfather was of Croatian descent and his wife came from an Italian family; as early as the tenth century A.D. the Venetian Republic controlled Split and made Dalmatia a place

where Italian speakers could live and make a living. Because the Croatians and Italians were Roman Catholic and used the same alphabet (Latin as opposed to the Serbian Cyrillic), the two groups lived together amicably. But the family lost much of their wealth during World War

Grandfather Juras' car factory, 1932

I when several of their business enterprises failed. Even so, automobile manufacturing remained into the 1930s one source of family income so that when I was a boy I visited a home that was opulent. That wealth trickled down to me in the form of those gold coins underneath my plate.

My mother was a dignified woman, domineering but also caring. She had five siblings, three sisters, Angelica, Rosarija, and my favorite aunt, Maritca, the oldest. Maritca was the only sibling to remain single and that meant that she could give my siblings and me a lot of attention, which some-times made up for my mother's formality. My mother also had two brothers — Milko and Vinco. All of her family remained in the Old Country after we left, and endured Communist rule.

Aunt Maritca and Uncle Milko in sidecar

In fact, one of my uncles, married to my mother's sister Angelica, was killed in the 1950s by the Communists, intentionally run over by a truck while walking through the center of Split.

My mother studied opera as a girl. With her family she took annual trips to Venice for shopping and to Vienna for the opera season. As an adult, she had the responsibility for overseeing the affairs of a large home, with four children and a successful husband. She had the help of a cook and nurse. My mother was living the same kind of life that she had experienced

Mike (left) with mother and Paul, 1935

in her parents' home. Because she had help in rearing the children, my mother usually did not know about my mischievous ways. For her, Paul and I were always "good boys."

Although her family maintained the conventions of genteel Croatian society, they acknowledged their responsibilities to the rest of society and were magnanimous with their affluence. I remember on several visits to my grandparents' home seeing a big dining area across the avenue outside the palace in which fifty to seventy-five of Split's less fortunate residents were eating food prepared by my grandparents, and children playing games on the floor after the meal. Today their neighborhood is filled with high-end shops and boutiques — the most fashionable shopping districts in the city. But in the 1930s it was the site of a family-run and family-funded soup kitchen that provided a form of charity that was more effective for many of the poor in Split than the assistance provided by the church or certainly the government.

The refined life my mother knew as a child, and continued to experience as an adult, meant that she always hoped she would return to her hometown. That hope disappeared when we eventually settled in New York City and she needed to work as a seamstress to help support the family. The difference between her life in Europe and her experience in the United States was enormous. But she also knew that returning was impossible after the war, because of Tito and the Communist rule in Yugoslavia. Even in her declining years, as a 90-year old woman, two years before her death, she spoke of wanting to join the United States military to fight the Communists. To her, Communist doctrine was incomprehensible — it was evil. To steal from the haves and give to the have-nots achieved nothing. It became counter-productive.

Mike's Grandmother & Grandfather,
Nevenka & Vincent Juras, ca. 1850

CHAPTER 4

Running with the Bulls in Bled

One of my fondest memories of early childhood before the war broke out was when we really went on vacation, unlike our feigned holiday in the spring of 1942. During the summer, which could be hot in Split, even if the Adriatic Sea kept temperatures comfortable at night, we traveled to the village of Bled in Slovenia, one of the most advanced provinces in Yugoslavia. In Split, temperatures in July and August would regularly soar to the 90s; in Bled, which is close to the Austrian border in the Julian Alps and about 1,700 feet above sea level, the air stayed in the 70s during the day and sometimes dipped into the 50s at night. Unfortunately for my father, he stayed in Split during most of the summer and kept the bank open. But like many upper class families, liberated from the routine of school, my mother took the children away for the summer.

Of course, we were not the only Europeans setting up residence in Bled during the summer. During the era of the first Yugoslavia, the Serbian ruling family, Karadjorgevic, made Bled their summer domicile. This was a tradition that the president of Communist Yugoslavia hijacked. In 1947 Josip Broz Tito built a summer house in Bled and another on the Adriatic Coast.

Tito's selection of Bled for his summer palace testifies to the region's enduring beauty. The village sits beside the glacial lake of the same

17

name. Since the mid-nineteenth century, when the Swiss naturalist and holistic healer, Arnold Rikli, visited Bled for his own recuperation, the town attracted tourists in search of health and relief. An island in the middle of the lake is the home of the Assumption of Mary Pilgrimage Church, another incentive for attracting visitors to the area.

The trip from Split to Bled was some 300 miles and our mode of transportation was a sleeper train. I did not sleep much on those trips because I was so excited to get there and resume my previous summer's explorations and games, and a bit of mischief.

Some of my most pleasant memories as a child were of those vacations in Bled. We stayed at the town's only good hotel, and as was my custom, I would go off on my own (at this point Paul, my future accomplice, was too young) and find something to do. Kids then did not have any technology to amuse themselves, but that only meant we needed to be creative. One summer day I went off to find the bulls. Bled was still largely rural, and numerous farms bordered the town. I had heard that bulls would react to someone if they waved a red flag. So I decided to try this experiment and see what kind of reaction I could provoke.

I had no trouble finding cows or bulls. But stimulating a response was another matter. At first, I waved the flag that I took from the hotel when no one was looking. But this proved ineffective. The bulls continued to lie in the corner of the barnyard. A few more waves and nothing. Maybe they were asleep. So I picked up a big stick and prodded one bull. This woke him up but still no reaction. Once awake, however, my wave of the flag did precisely what I had heard would happen. The bull sprang to its feet and took off after me. Thank goodness I was blessed with speed and my legs took me as fast as they could away from the charging bull, which at one point felt like it was breathing down my neck.

I liked to think that I did not scare easily. Somehow I came to believe that if I was afraid of small things I would fear everything. When I arrived back at the hotel, out of breath and dripping with sweat, I was excited enough to tell my parents about this adventure. Maybe I was not afraid because I did not know how much danger I had been in. So I blurted out about the fun I had at the barn and proceeded to explain my performance in front of the bulls. Only my father laughed.

Little did my parents or I know then that within a few years, when the government of Yugoslavia fell and then the Axis powers invaded Croatia, my parents and siblings would be following my example of running from danger. The threat posed by Italian and Croatian Fascist soldiers and Communist forces would not only end our summer trips to Bled but also force us to use all means, both speedy and savvy, to escape the wide carnage that enveloped the area.

Mike's parents, Nevenka and Branko Novakovic, 1938

CHAPTER 5

I Wanted to Be Like Uncle Vlado

My father's generation of the Novakovics was the first that did not send a son into the priesthood of the Serbian Orthodox Church. For over four centuries my father's family had served as priests, some as bishops, and other family members went into the military. Obviously, someone could make more money in another line of work. While my father and his ten brothers remained active in the church as members, at the start of the twentieth century, they had many more opportunities to make a living, even as confused and turbulent as Yugoslavia was. My uncles went into careers in medicine, the military, and government. One served briefly as an assistant to the prime minister.

My favorite uncle was Vlado, who at one point held the rank of a commander in the Royal Yugoslav Army. These armed forces were responsible for the initial military resistance to the Italian invasion of Yugoslavia. My uncle's unit, which included about 5,000 soldiers under his command from the district of Knin, was one of the few that persisted in fighting the Axis powers. The King had awarded him the title of ***vojvoda***,

Mike's Uncle Vlado Novakovic in military uniform.

translated simply as *leader*, but also a designation that included a status comparable in power and prestige to a duke. Shortly before the Italian invasion, the Royal Army collapsed, thanks to internal divisions along the perennially divisive ethnic lines of the Balkans peoples. In this case, the Croats and Slovenes refused to defend a Serb-dominated resistance movement whose aim was to preserve the rule of a Serbian king in Yugoslavia. Parochial outlooks prevailed.

Mike's Uncle Vlado

I remember vividly one of the few times that Uncle Vlado visited my family during the initial skirmishes of the war. He arrived with several trucks filled with at least two dozen of his soldiers and many more on foot. He was in uniform and fully armed — pistols on his waist and grenades on his chest. He sat down in our parlor and I ran over to sit in his lap. When I began to point at and touch the pistols he did not seem to mind. But when my hands reached the grenades, he said: "Michael, don't touch those!"

Of course, as a little boy who liked to play games of combat, to have a real live officer, my uncle, in full uniform, drab olive in color with accents of red on his cap, and carrying weapons, was a thrill. I knew some of the consequences of explosives and guns — we had been living with the sights and sounds of war for some time. But my desire to play could get the better of me and as a boy of nine a gun could still be a toy. That notion soon ended.

My ability to create mischief on the forces I perceived as the "bad guys" developed early in the war and was evident soon after my uncle's visit. The first stages of the Italian occupation were in place and the invading military was using one of the city's hospitals to treat their wounded soldiers. Because of Italy's historic presence in Split and the province of Dalmatia, some of the Croats in the city were comfortable with the Italian soldiers; for most of the Dalmatian population, Italian was a second or third language. But Serbs, like my family, were royalists who opposed Fascists and Communists equally. For that reason, I was determined to create headaches for these unwelcome soldiers.

My brother, Paul and I, along with a friend in the neighborhood, established a relationship with several of the Italian soldiers in the

hospital. This was also one of the first indications of my entrepreneurial instincts. The soldiers would give us money to buy them cigarettes which were forbidden in the hospital. We made a little money and so were inclined to go along at first. The soldiers would lower a small box, tied to a string, down from one of their windows to us on the street. We would take the money and then find cigarettes.

Mike, age 9 (left) and Paul, age 8, in the mountains of Slovenia, 1939

We received a very modest tip for our efforts. At first, we started small. They would give us a few lira and we would send up five or six cigarettes. Over time, the demand increased and we were exchanging as many as 100 cigarettes on each transaction. Obviously, the box had become a lot bigger by then. Had our parents known what we were up to, they would have disapproved. But they had a lot more to worry about and generally trusted us not to get into trouble.

Eventually, we decided to turn the Italians' trust into a small act of vengeance. On one of our exchanges, we decided not to put cigarettes in the box but a good sized pile of horse dung. The soldiers should probably have figured out that something was amiss once they began to pull the box back to their window; not that many people have held horse dung, but they can well imagine that it weighs more than dried tobacco rolled in smoking paper. Anyhow, as soon as the Italians began to draw the box to their window, we ran. When they saw what they had purchased, they began to yell at us, using lots of Italian curse words and indecent hand gestures. Of course, we took off, doubled up with laughter and proud of our accomplishment.

We did not return to the hospital as vendors of cigarettes but my brother and I did determine to keep up the mischief. The Italians had about fifty trucks parked in one section of Split and we noticed that they had only one soldier guarding the entire fleet. At first we had fun letting air out of the trucks tires. Because air pumps were in short supply and not mechanized, the task of filling the tires back up was not as easy as it is today. But soon the thrill of this venture wore off and we were game for something more disruptive.

So I decided I would try to set the trucks on fire, again an indication of how my age prevented me from calculating the possible consequences of my conduct. We put boxes underneath the trucks and set them on fire. Our first attempts were unsuccessful. We did not realize what success would mean until one of the trucks actually caught fire and its fuel tank blew up. At this point our prank caught the attention of the Italian officials. My small band of conspirators and I not only had to run from that blast but had to keep a very low profile. If caught, it would have been instant execution.

I am sure my parents did not know that I was responsible for blowing up the truck. This incident was not appreciated by the Italian Army and they tried very hard to find the perpetrator, but it remained a secret. My Uncle Vlado would have been proud.

CHAPTER 6

On the Move Again

Although Croatia during the 1930s experienced a variety of conflicts, thanks to the historic antagonisms of the region, life in Split
for me as a boy was remarkably routine and calm — too much so at
times. The city had witnessed various administrations going all the way
back to the Roman Empire and as an important port and link to trade
routes, the people of the city and its surrounding area knew how to go
about their business no matter who was in power. For me this meant
that once I turned six, I headed off to school, not one of my favorite
things to do.

As was common throughout Europe, the school system in Split
divided children between those headed toward professions and those
who would go into trades or manual work. I fell into the category of
professions due to my family's social standing and received a classical
education that included Latin. Students going into trades followed a
practical or technical course of learning. At the time, I had no idea
about a career (except when Uncle Vlado visited). I did have definite
ideas about the boredom of schoolwork.

The problem for me (and I guess for my teachers) was that I did not
like to be forced to do anything. I ran everywhere and loved to sprint
here and there wherever my curiosity took me. I was fast (and when I
eventually enrolled at Syracuse University in the era of the well-known

football player, Jim Brown, the track coaches wanted me to join the team). But in the classroom such speed needed to be harnessed and my physical energy became a liability to my potential as a student. In fact, teachers expected us to sit up straight, cross our arms, and repeat any number of lessons in math or reading. Math was easy to me then and also later when I was a student in Argentina, New York City, or intelligence school for the U.S. Air Force. I also excelled at geography, which was a great asset for the rest of my nomadic life. But sitting still and doing nothing was a problem.

To relieve these constraining conditions I employed different strategies. In the classroom itself I often made faces at the teacher when she was writing on the chalk board. I guess this made me the class clown. Other students seemed to enjoy these antics. But, of course, when the teacher turned around to look for the source of the disturbance, I would resume the required position with perfect posture and arms crossed — the "model" student.

I also used some of my learning to create a diversion from the calm and unending regimen of the primary school day. I am still not sure how I did it, but I figured out a way to take ammonia and mix it with sulfur (I think I used matches), let the concoction "brew" for several days, and then unleashed the foul odor in one of

Paul (left) and Mike in front of their Father's Buick,

the school's hallways by unscrewing the bottle's cap. It was a terrible smell and all of the teachers were quite upset. Of course, I had to act like I didn't know what had happened, and the foul smell helped — I did not have to fake turning my head and holding my nose to avoid the stink. But inside I was giddy. And no one ever figured out who had set off the stink bomb. Not even my younger brother, Paul, who was also in primary school, ever learned that I was the one behind the stink bomb.

At home I was also up to no good. The piano under the Picasso was a problem. My parents owned a large Picasso painting which hung on the wall behind the grand piano. One day I took my toy dart gun, aimed at an animal in the painting, and shot a nice half inch hole into the canvas. Not good, but I was able to fix it so that it was not readily visible. During the war, when the Fascist police ransacked our house, the painting was stolen. There is some justice because whoever has the painting now, has a wounded Picasso.

I was subjected to the finer aspects of Croatian civilization, which meant piano lessons. Thanks to my mother's musical training, she wanted to expose me to the joy and beauty of music and thought learning to read music by playing the piano would be a worthwhile activity. I dreaded those lessons. Again, my boundless energy got the better of me, my piano teacher, and my mother's best intentions. Perhaps if I had stayed with the lessons long enough I could have learned how to "sprint" with my fingers across the keyboard. But at that stage of my life, I was only interested in exercising my legs.

As it turned out, the war would be my way of escaping the rigors of sitting still. I distinctly remember when the bombs fell near our house one early morning the day before the Axis invasion of Croatia in 1941 I thought to myself with some joy and relief that I would no longer have to submit to the leg-numbing exercises of sitting at the piano and learning to play scales. At the time, a child like me was much more interested in the adventures presented by soldiers and gunshots than the ordinary task of going to school and practicing the piano. Only a few months later I realized how serious was the nature of the armed conflict in Croatia and the rest of Europe and how devastating the disruption of war would be for teachers, students, piano players, and mothers, who wanted their children to grow up to enjoy the music and art that had once made Europe a civilized place.

All that training must have done some good, for now we subscribe to the Philadelphia Orchestra and enjoy it immensely. Our grandson, Nikolas, who is 18 years old is an accomplished piano player. My mother would be proud.

CHAPTER 7

War Hits Home

Until I turned eight, my life in Split was fairly routine and pleasant. During the school year I went to class. In the summers we went on vacation, and at home my siblings and I followed the instruction of cooks and nurses. Around the town I played with friends and siblings. Life in Yugoslavia, however, was by no means quite so idyllic in the years leading up to 1941. The Kingdom of Yugoslavia had failed, Croatian independence movements were flexing their muscles, and to the south of Yugoslavia, Mussolini was sending his forces into Albania and Greece to prove to Hitler that Italians were capable of occupying other lands without the Führer's permission. In point of fact, Mussolini proved just the opposite. When his forces invaded Greece on October 28, 1940, Greek defenders gave the Allies their first victory on land during World War II. This meant that Hitler would have to send German soldiers to do what Mussolini could not.

Being surrounded by war and contending armed forces meant that I became very skilled at discerning when planes were headed toward us. A very early memory comes from a walk that I was taking with my aunt Maritca when I first saw military planes. Their size and noise mesmerized me. I forced my aunt to stop and gaze up at the spectacle with me. While I looked on with a sense of childish awe, my aunt said, "Michael, some day you will have to rescue us." Little did she know how prophetic that remark would be and I never forgot it. Throughout the rest of the war, and even later in my military career, I invariably heard fighter planes and bombers approaching even before the town's sirens alerted residents to head to the nearest shelter.

One night in 1941, however, I was not so alert. My brother, Paul, and I were sleeping soundly in our bedroom, in our comfortable and elegant third and fourth floor apartments above the bank where my father worked. Without any warning, bombs exploding within some 150 feet of our home, woke us from our sleep. We had no idea what was going on. We had even less time to figure out the nature of the attack since my brother was soon screaming and holding his leg. When my parents examined him, they immediately saw blood flowing from a wound caused by shrapnel. They also saw that parts of the ceiling in our room had fallen to the floor. Our home was a mess, with debris scattered about after the explosion. The situation prevented us from taking Paul to the hospital. My father knew a physician who lived close by and came to our home to remove the shrapnel. There was no anesthesia.

We spent the rest of the night in a bomb shelter. My parents had prepared for the war by having a bomb shelter built in the basement of our building, complete with logs and sandbags to fortify the space against explosions, storing a little bit of food and water, and luminos — a crude lamp made from a glass container holding oil, a piece of cork floating in the oil, and a wick pointing up through the cork that held the flame. Our home sat on a point of land overlooking Split's harbor. Today it holds the offices for the French, Dutch, and English consulates. A large wall reinforced the waterfront. Luckily, the bomb landed on the sea side of that wall. If it had dropped on our side, I don't think we would have survived.

The attack, as it turned out, was part of the Italian effort to take control of the province of Dalmatia. It was a form of intimidation to subdue the region. But because of the ongoing conflicts in Yugoslavia among the Fascists (Ustashi), Communists (Partisans), and Chetniks, those loyal to the monarchy, it could have been an attack by either of the first two. The Ustashi, or Croatian Revolutionary Movement were particularly strong in Split. As Fascists, they would eventually cooperate with the Italians and Germans during the Axis occupation of Yugoslavia. Because my father was Serbian and loyal to the king, he was a marked man by both the Ustashi and the Partisans.

The injury to Paul and the destruction of part of our home left my parents with a serious dilemma. They were aware of the instability of Yugoslavia, but they had been living with that uncertainty for much of their adult lives. They also knew that Hitler and Mussolini were, by 1941, already invading other counties to the east and south in their quest for dominance of Europe and even the world. Now my parents were keenly alert to the direct danger that they and their children faced from the war that was engulfing the rest of Europe. But what were their choices? Remaining in Split was unsafe, but was it any more dangerous than some other part of Europe? My brother and I had little understanding of this dilemma. But after Paul's wounds we did have first-hand knowledge of the threat that war posed to ordinary residents in places like Split.

CHAPTER 8

Downsized

After the bombing that wounded my brother, life in Split was increasingly unsafe. A halfway solution to my parent's problem was to relocate the family to our villa outside the city limits of Split. This villa was a place my parents used on weekends for a rural respite and access to the Adriatic Sea. It was only a ten-minute drive from our primary residence and a desirable piece of property, so much so that the government of Yugoslavia would use part of our land to start constructing a museum for the famous Croatian sculptor, Ivan Meštrovic, about whom I will have more to say later.

My parents had additional reasons for seeking a place to live outside the city. The Ustashi, an intense and powerful Croatian militia, were increasing their push for Croatian independence. That did not bode well for my Serbian father since they also were known for their ethnic cleansing policies. The word **ustashi** itself means revolt or insurrection, not the best name for a party intent on establishing order in a particular society.

The Ustashi's origins date back to the nineteenth century and the rise of Croatian nationalism. At the time, Croatian nationalists desired a united Balkan region that would be independent from the Habsburgs in Austria and purified from Serbian and Muslim elements. This outlook considered all the peoples of the region to be descendants of a common Slav stock, some of whom had been converted, against their will, by Eastern Orthodox Christians (Serbs) and the Turks (Muslims). Croatian nationalists thought of their land as the chief bastion of western civilization and the true faith — Roman Catholicism.

In the twentieth century the Ustashi became the principal opponents of the Kingdom of Yugoslavia, and their primary means of opposition was terror. The leader of the Ustashi, who also became the head of Croatia during World War II, at the encouragement and support of Mussolini, was Ante Pavelic, later known as the "butcher of the Balkans." Born in 1889, he joined a nationalist organization at a young age and would later resurrect youth movements to generate converts to the Ustashi cause. His attempts to undermine the Yugoslavian government were partly responsible for King Alexander's decision to abolish the constitution and institute a "dictatorship." That change also forced Pavelic into exile, first to Hungary and then to Italy where Mussolini had recruited him to cultivate a Croatian Fascist movement in Yugoslavia.

The success of Pavelic's endeavors contributed directly to the civil wars that dogged Yugoslavia during my days as a boy. In 1932, the year I was born, Pavelic masterminded a Ustashi invasion of Croatia through the port city of Zadar, about 80 miles north of Split. In motorboats, these revolutionaries crossed the Adriatic Sea from Italy and after initial success ran into superior forces in the Velebit Mountains. Many stories circulated later, sometimes indicative of the ethnic hatred that afflicted both sides, that Pavelic was also influential in the assassination of King Alexander in 1934 in Marsailles, at the hands of a Bulgarian agent recruited for the deed by the Ustashi. Unfortunately, reason, fairness, logic and human dignity did not prevail on both sides.

By 1939, the Yugoslavian government was trying to remain neutral in the emerging war between the Axis powers and the Allies. Croatian nationalists, however, welcomed German pressure for Yugoslavia to join the Tripartite Pact of 1939 which would have placed Yugoslavia on the side of the Axis. Yugoslavia remained neutral until 1941 when it finally capitulated to Hitler's iron fist. On March 26, 1941, the Yugoslav air force attempted a coup against Pavelic. It failed. Then pro-German sentiments in Zagreb and elsewhere toppled the government of King Alexander. As a result, Pavelic gained his wish for independence from Serbian dominance. The Germans then crushed the anti-German uprising, occupied Zagreb, and allowed Pavelic to return to Croatia as the leader of the Fascist government.

German occupation did not wipe out Serbian opposition, however. In fact, one of the more remarkable incidents in World War II came in 1944 when Serbians, loyal to the old monarchy, assisted the United States in rescuing 512 downed U.S. airmen behind Nazi lines in the mountains of Yugoslavia, first by providing shelter to the airmen and then working with United States military officials secretly to arrange for an amazing airlift that would escape the Germans' detection. American agents from the Office of Strategic Services, precursor to the CIA, worked with a Serbian guerilla leader, General Draza Mihailovic, to carry out this vast rescue mission. It was so secret that the British and United States officials prevented word of the rescue from being released to the wider public (mainly to avoid taking sides in the conflict-riddled antagonisms of the Balkans during the difficult negotiations between East and West after World War II).

Although the fall of Yugoslavia was the result of the German and Italian occupation forces, Croatian nationalism was an ever-present threat in Split and the surrounding region. Members of the Ustashi not only wanted to be rid of Serbian dominance but they also desired an ethnically and religiously pure Croatia. The full meaning of that desire became clear after Pavelic returned from exile and ethnic cleansing began at the Serbian village of Gudovac in Bosnia-Herzegovina. My father realized that a Serbian, whose family had been part of the Serbian Orthodox priesthood, was in danger. The Ustashi would eventually target Jews, Gypsies and Orthodox priests for removal from Croatia. Reports state that apparently at Pavelic's direction, during World War II, up to 30,000 Jews, 29,000 Gypsies, and between 300,000 and 600,000 Serbs lost their lives according to historians' estimates.

The problem with our villa as a place of safe retreat was that the only way to travel there was in my father's prized Mercury. In that car, my family stuck out like a sore thumb; we probably would have stood out in any car, but that new luxury vehicle was a dead giveaway. So my parents decided to return to Split and go into hiding. A very generous Croatian family, a distant cousin of my mother, took us in and for several weeks we lived in the attic of this family's home. We did not venture outside the attic for anything. The only way to pass the time was to play board and card games, or read and pray.

We could not hide in an attic for the rest of the war. And we had no idea how the events of the civil war or the World War would turn out. I was largely oblivious to the greater significance of these developments for my family and our citizenship in Yugoslavia. But I knew enough to understand that the place where I had grown up was no longer home. Anarchy prevailed. It ruled the country. Mob rule. Bloodshed everywhere.

CHAPTER 9

The Last Straw

The occupation of Yugoslavia by Italian forces under Mussolini would not appear to be the most promising of developments for the city of Split or my family. But the Italian presence actually provided a measure of relief and allowed us to come out of hiding. Once the Italians invaded Croatia we tried very briefly to return to life as normal.

Two years prior to our departure from Croatia, the Kingdom of Yugoslavia enacted a treaty known as the Cvetkovic-Macek agreement. It went into effect on August 23, 1939 and was named for the Yugoslav Prime Minister Dragiša Cvetkovic, a Serb, and Vladko Macek, a Croat politician. This policy established the Banovina of Croatia as a sub-state within Yugoslavia which would include as many ethnic Croats as possible. It was a major victory for Croatian nationalists who had opposed their inclusion within Yugoslavia since the end of World War I. The agreement also had in view the territories of Bosnia and Herzegovina, which would be divided along ethnic lines between the Serbs and Croats. Closer to home, this agreement enabled the Ustashi to flex their muscles of intimidation and thuggery against Serbs and other residents outside the Roman Catholic Church.

When the Axis powers of Germany and Italy decided to annex Yugoslavia, the traditional province of Dalmatia, the region that included Split, became part of Italy. The new Italian policy divided the Govern-

ment of Dalmatia into three districts: Zara, Split, and Kotor. The man
in charge was Giuseppe Bastianini, who reported directly to Mussolini.
He was clearly a Fascist and had worked to establish terrorist organizations that helped the Fascists come to power. But because Dalmatia
had historic ties to the Republic of Venice, the Italian language and
culture were familiar to people who lived along the Dalmatian coast and
for Serbians like my father and for those like my mother, who had Italian roots, the occupation by Italy was slightly less threatening than rule
by Croatian nationalists who were also Fascists.

Coming out of the attic, however, looked foolish a few weeks later
when the Italian government arrested my father. At the same time that
the Italian soldiers took my father, they also ransacked our home and
stole our most valuable possessions. What dumbfounded me more than
the loss of gold coins were the items the soldiers took simply as a form
of intimidation. They took my toys — lead soldiers that I played with
frequently — a stamp collection, and a wooden saber. The only value
of these possessions was sentimental. But the soldiers wanted to hurt us
and show they were in charge. Instilling as much terror as they could
was one persuasive way of doing so. I was particularly attached to that
saber. During one outing when I was playing outside with it, the local
bully (much older than I) took it from me. Rather than going inside to
complain to my mother, as I had many times with this boy, this time I
went right up to him, looked him in the eye, told him he couldn't have
it, and grabbed it back. From that moment, he and his friends never
bothered me again. It helped that my sister Gordana (older than me by
about four years) was my enforcer who regularly defended me from kids
who wanted to take advantage because of their older age or larger size.
They knew she would also get them. She was strong.

The reason for the Italian imprisonment of my father was arbitrary.
He had done nothing wrong, but as a member of the upper class, a man
of means, and a Serbian of royalist sympathies, he was precisely the
kind of Yugoslavian that the Italians wanted to eliminate. The lengths

to which my father was intimidated were evident to him while he was in jail. At the same time, the Italians had also rounded up the son of our neighbor, an older adolescent, only 18, who was always kind to my brother and me. The authorities took him to the square at the back of our apartment complex, executed him, and left him there by the wall. His body lay there for two days before anyone had the courage to arrange for burial. This was one of the very few times when events concerned me directly; the death of our neighbor suggested a similar fate awaited my family. Rounding up local citizens and beating or killing them was a common technique for instilling fear in the population and another indication that during World War II, using the memorable words of Major Heinrich Strasser in the movie *Casablanca*, "Human life is cheap."

Fortunately, the local Italian prefect and keeper of the jail that held my father was not an ideologue. That meant that he was looking out for himself as much as he was a devotee of Fascism or Italian nationalism. My mother, with some counsel from a family friend, decided to approach the prefect and offer him a bribe. She paid the ransom in gold coins, the first indication of the power that currency would have for our escape from our own home town. I don't remember how much she offered, but it was enough to liberate my father after one hellish night in jail. It was nerve-racking for us at home but more so for him behind bars. I later discovered he was scheduled for execution the next morning.

Although Dalmatia was part of Italy as of April 1941, the Ustashi were still vigorous and numerous. Since the Italians and Ustashi were both Fascists, they cooperated on a number of levels. But they were also at odds, thanks to the Ustashi's traditional desire for an independent Croatia. Just outside of Split, I remember seeing a place that the Italians had used to execute some of the most obstreperous Croatian nationalists. One morning while I was going about my routine, I discovered just how truculent the Ustashi still were under Italian rule.

After leaving our neighbor's attic, I started to attend the local school again. The schools had yet to close, which they would later in the month. On one of my morning trips to class, sprinting through the streets as was my custom, I heard a shot and immediately realized that the bullet was meant for me. It was amazing. Someone was shooting at me. That someone was a member of the Ustashi who was casually sitting on a doorstep with his rifle. Obviously, I kept running. I eventually arrived at school and had no further incident that day.

When I returned home that day, I told my parents about the shooting. When my mother spoke with her parents, my grandmother advised that we should leave Split immediately. If my mother was going to see her children survive, she and my father would need to find another home for us. Since my mother was very attached to her family, this was the encouragement she needed even to consider leaving her homeland. She could leave with her mother's approval. Clearly there were many Croats that did not fit the Ustashi mold and opposed to what was going on.

CHAPTER 10

Rendezvous in Trieste

In 1942 Trieste was not necessarily any more stable than Croatia. But it was for all intents and purposes part of Italy and so a step closer to the Allied forces which would eventually defeat the Italian army by way of a difficult invasion of Italy from the south. Our family decided to start our sojourn there partly because it was the closest Italian city to us. Plus, my parents were familiar with the city. When we arrived in Trieste, without my father, we took rooms at the Hotel Esplanada, a grand establishment, the finest hotel in the city, where my parents had stayed many times before the war. Since it was familiar to them, my father and mother agreed that we would wait for my father there. In an era before good communication, a fixed meeting point was the best they could do. My mother had to hope that nothing would deter my father on his way to Trieste. Given the situation, that was a leap of faith.

For almost six centuries, since 1382, Trieste, a small sliver of land in the northwest part of the Istrian peninsula, had been under Austrian protection, though most Italians preferred to think of the Duke of Austria as an oppressor. In fact, one of Italy's reasons for entering World War I had been to recover both the cities of Trento and Trieste, which were populated by many Italians. After World War I, the Habsburg Dynasty ceded both cities back to the Italians, an act which marked the last gasp of the Austro-Hungarian Empire. The rest of the peninsula remained part of Croatia. No matter Trieste's past or future, we were not planning on remaining there. We simply needed a place to stay until my father managed to leave Split.

It took him almost two weeks before he felt sufficiently secure to take the same boat and route that we had taken to Trieste. My mother had actually wanted to return to Split before my father was able to leave. Her mother was sick and she wanted to see her, maybe even for the last time, since we did not know if we would ever return to Split. Because these ships ran back and forth regularly between Trieste, Pula, and Split, the crew or passengers would often take messages between the cities. Before the advent of long distance telephone service, this was the only way for my parents to communicate about when they were traveling, where we were staying, or whether or not to go back to Split. I am still amazed that my father had no problem finding us, but money talks.

Like us, he needed to travel light. He did bring two suitcases, each weighing about thirty pounds. They were filled with gold coins like the ones we had hidden underneath our clothes and in our few bags when we left Split. This was the gold that my grandfather on my mother's side had hidden at home. By the time he reached Trieste he had only one suitcase, which was taxing to carry by itself. When he crossed the border between Croatia and Italy, the guards discovered the contents of his luggage. His only way out of the predicament was to offer the head guard a bribe. In return for half the gold, my father would be able to take the other suitcase with him and stay on course for Trieste. By the time he found us at the Esplanada, the relief of being reunited with his wife and children more than offset the disappointment of losing the suitcase of gold. Even with just the one suitcase, carrying around all of that gold was very difficult.

Although Trieste, in Northeast Italy, was not in the line of the Allies' advance through Italy from the south, the city was still hardly peaceful during our brief stay in 1942. Even before the war, Fascists had begun to attack Jews and their property; the Jewish population in Trieste had been the third largest in Italy overall. During our stay, in July 1942, anti-Semitic inspired attacks on Trieste's Great Synagogue by Fascist squads and sympathetic mobs destroyed that hallowed place.

Another source of unrest in the city during our stay was the presence of Yugoslav Partisan movements which opposed Italy's invasion of Croatia and Yugoslavia. Only with the German occupation of Trieste in September 1943 did a measure of order emerge. Offsetting this false sense of tranquility was the Nazi decision in 1944 to build a concentration camp in the outskirts of Trieste, the only one on Italian soil. Around 3,000 Jews, South Slavs, Serbs, and Italian anti-Fascists were killed in this camp, while thousands of others were imprisoned before being transferred to other concentration camps and the gas chambers. Trieste was hardly a safe place to hide.

There was also great tumult among the Italian Fascists, Nazis, and Yugoslav Partisans during our time in the city. Though far from one of World War II's major fronts, it was marked by air raids, explosions, and ambulance sirens. The city is situated in a region that is geologically unique because of the many caves in the surrounding hills. The Trieste plateau has roughly 1,500 caves. One of the most famous of these natural hollows is the Grotta Gigante, the largest tourist cave in the world, big enough to contain the structure of St. Peter's Basilica. In the city of Trieste itself the municipal authorities took one of these caves and modified it to construct a shelter for citizens during the war. Over time the cave, now a system of tunnels, acquired the name, Kleines Berlin, owing to the German expansion of the tunnel system after their 1943 occupation of the Adriatic coast. One part of the tunnel was accessible to residents of the city, the other was only open to German soldiers. In the common area were benches, first aid rooms, and toilet facilities. The German part, added after we left Trieste, had big rooms and offices for the SS (Schutzstaffel) troops and their officers.

My family and I became familiar with the municipal side of those tunnels, which had three points of access along the via Fabio Severo. Often before the sirens sounded to alert residents of an impending air raid,

I would hear the hum of four-engine bomber aircraft and we would run from our rooms at the hotel to the tunnel's entrance. Over time, I became especially adept at detecting the sound of military aircraft. Even if I was sleeping, the low, humming sound of the planes roused me from slumber and I would wake up the rest of the family so we could run for the cave. As the fastest, I arrived first, of course. But since my parents would split up the children to keep the entire family from being destroyed in one of these raids — Deana and I went with my mother, and Paul and Gordana stayed with my father — my speed in this case was more of a hindrance than a help to my parents' management of their children.

I do not recall if my parents had any misgivings about leaving Split for Trieste. Our home in Yugoslavia had almost been destroyed and my brother Paul had already been wounded during the initial air raids of the war and I had been shot at. Now we faced a similar predicament. Even if our accommodations in Trieste were the best we would experience during the entire war, the need to seek shelter in the city's tunnels as often as we did must have worried my parents. Obviously, we could not return to Split. But how long could we reasonably stay in Trieste? Compounding our dilemma was the historic conflict between Italian and Yugoslavian claims on the city. Even if German occupation made Trieste unsafe for refugees like us, local divisions between Italians and Slavs made an extended stay there impossible even though, by this time, we had papers stating that we were Italian citizens.

CHAPTER 11

Rendezvous with the Allies

Trieste, like my home town of Split, was a disputed municipality. After the Austro-Hungarian Empire returned the city to Italian control, a condition for Italy's joining the Entente Powers during World War I against the Central Powers, tensions in Trieste shifted to conflict between Italy and Yugoslavia. Irredentists in Italy, always hoping to restore Italian rule to all areas where an Italian-speaking community existed, were not content with territories ceded by World War I treaties. Large parts of Yugoslavia, especially those along the Adriatic coast, such as Dalmatia, were desirable to Irredentists. Mussolini had appealed to nationalism to justify his 1930s invasions of territories outside Italy. These conditions made rivalry between Italy and Yugoslavia inevitable. One of the casualties of this conflict was Trieste. If Italy was going to expand its claims in the Julian region, Yugoslav nationalists would fight back by trying to take back Trieste and other parts of historic Slovenian lands from Italians.

This conflict between Italy and Yugoslavia was largely responsible for the warfare my family and I experienced during our two-month stay in Trieste. In fact, after the Axis powers occupied Yugoslavia in the spring of 1941, Yugoslav resistance movements emerged to oppose the Axis powers by deploying forces in Trieste. One of these groups was the Chetniks, a movement led largely by officers in the former Yugoslav military who defended both ideologically and physically the restoration of the pre-war Kingdom of Yugoslavia. Another form of resistance came from the Communists, also known as Partisans. Tito was the leader of the Slovenian Partisans, who were divided ethnically and linguistically along the Italian and Slovenian lines. Not only did these groups oppose the Italian Fascist government's expansion into Yugoslavia, but various independent anti-communist bodies emerged to fight the insurgence of Communists.

The presence of these factions meant that Trieste was surrounded by, if not subject to, ad hoc instances of armed conflict. From the summer of 1942 on, Partisans raided Italian strongholds and Mussolini's forces retaliated, sometimes by burning the cities that Communists had controlled. Late in 1942, the Italian and Slovenian Partisans met in Trieste secretly to coordinate their resistance activities. The Italian government tried to suppress these efforts, which meant that the city of Trieste was not only subject to armed aggression (from various ideological quarters) but also under close surveillance. It was not a safe place to be even if Chetniks enjoyed sympathy and some support from Trieste's middle class and intellectuals, which included my parents. The word chaos could have originated here.

For these reasons, my mother and father decided to leave northern Italy and head south. The hope was that as the Allies, who were gearing up for an invasion in the South, proceeded north, we might find more favorable conditions than the ones that existed amidst the fight between Fascists and Communists. Obviously, our primary desire was safety and food. If we could find a city that the Allies had occupied, we might also finally enjoy a peaceful existence and determine what to do for the remainder of the war and maybe, if we survived, with the rest of our lives. The city that my parents chose for our next stop in war-torn Italy was Ancona, another municipality on the Adriatic coast, about 350 miles southwest of Trieste, almost due West across the Adriatic Sea from Split.

Our mode of transportation was humble but it turned out to be good preparation for our stay in Ancona. My father arranged with the engineer of a small train, used to transport cattle, to gain passage for the family. We had no tickets, there was no conductor to take them. The small car that carried us for that 350 mile excursion was empty of livestock but reeked of cows and their refuse. It would normally have taken several hours, but because of the chaos of war and tight security with various check points the trip seemed never-ending. For me, a boy of eleven, the ride, though certainly lacking the luxury of the trains that took us to Bled, was an adventure, at least for the first several hours. For my parents and older sister, Deana, then eighteen years old, it was as barbaric as it was unsettling. The odors and filth were dreadful, but we lived.

When we finally arrived in Ancona my parents looked for a place off the beaten path, so that we could keep a low profile as befitting our precarious legal status. They found a villa outside town on one of the surrounding hillsides. My father had a friend there, through his business connections, who owned a large estate. The friend had moved to northern Italy to flee the conflict that was building as the Allies moved the front from the South to the North. This left the villa completely open to us. The servants who worked the farm had not left and were living in the out buildings when we arrived. It was a grand place, with a formal ballroom, much more than we needed. That grandeur would later become a problem for us.

Today Ancona is a beautiful seaport town of more than 100,000 people which attracts many tourists. The Ancona Cathedral sits on the Guasco Hill, overlooking the city's port, and offers amazing views of Ancona and the Adriatic coast. The wooden roof of the 11th century Cathedral is in the shape of an upside-down boat and its most obvious feature is the 12-sided cupola. The Cathedral is actually built on the site of an ancient temple dedicated to Venus and you can still see some of the ruins underneath the church. However, in war torn Europe, we were struggling for our lives, and soon discovered that Ancona was as vulnerable as Trieste, though the sources of armed conflict were different.

On one of our first days at the Luxardo estate I had another direct encounter with the violence of war. I was out walking along the road on one of the surrounding hills, exploring the terrain. I would often go out into the hills in search of food and watch the war, the planes carrying and dropping bombs, explosions and churning smoke, and the movements of troops. On this particular day, I watched as several United States fighter planes strafed a train that was running through the valley. When the last plane approached the train, one of the cars blew up — probably carrying ammunition, the obvious object of the attack. It threw up a large flame and dark clouds of smoke. Beyond the explosion I could see all of the planes except for the last one. That pilot had not been able to avoid the ball of fire, and had crashed on the other side of the tracks, an unforgettable sight.

I also roamed the area looking for an optimal perch. All around me were Italian and German soldiers who were used to going about their business with local civilians nearby. I was no bother to them and was fast becoming accustomed to their presence. But I was not used to seeing United States fighter pilots — flying Mustangs — who would daily search for targets of opportunity. Several other planes, flying very, very low and at slow speeds, had come through the area and shot at the Axis soldiers. They shot at anything that moved. (I identified the aircraft after the war.)

As I was walking and watching the tactics of the pilots I noticed that one of the planes was headed for me. He was also shooting in my direction. I could have decided, like Cary Grant in the Alfred Hitchcock movie, **North by Northwest**, to run and try to find cover behind a cropping of stones. But I did not choose to use my speed. Instead I stood, looked up, and waved at the pilot. He must have been flying so slowly by that time. I can still remember his helmet, mask, and goggles. That is how close he came and how alert I was to the imminent danger. What really stands out is that at the very moment that I waved, he stopped firing. If I had run, I think he would have kept shooting at me.

Did my decision to wave to the pilot save my life? I will never know for sure, but at the time it certainly seemed that my friendliness was responsible for halting his fire. That gesture in hindsight might seem odd and naïve. But in this case, my wave to the pilot was also an indication of my admiration for the American soldiers. Even when they bombed the surrounding area, my family and I were strangely confident that they would not hit us because they were the good guys, fighting to save people like us from the Germans, Italians, and Communists. But on this day I put the American pilot to a test that strained his good intentions. That was a close call. I can't believe what I did but I did it.

CHAPTER 12

Ancona: No Safe Harbor

As we settled into life at Luxardo Estate, we tried to resume some sense of normalcy in our lives. We had little to do beyond looking for food, preparing meals, and keeping a low profile to avoid attention.

During the five months we stayed in Ancona, the specter of war drew closer. In fact, we heard bombs exploding both very near and far, and they were much more frequent than anything we had experienced to date. The Allies bombed the city daily. Waves of planes would fly over and we had some minutes to find shelter. However, another type of attack was more dangerous. Those attacks were from the sea — allied destroyers shelled the coastal strategic targets. Since the town was only a thirty minute walk from our residence, the bombs often felt like they were directed at us as much as the city's port, railways, and industrial facilities.

My brother Paul and I were always trying to make up games to fill the time. In Ancona, we decided to keep count of the bomb explosions. Our final count of air raids and bombardments from the sea for our stay in Ancona numbered approximately 115. When bombs dropped from aircraft we were frightened of course, but at least we had time, especially thanks to my heightened sense of hearing. And since we were outside the city, we were not near the targets of ship yards and munitions facilities. Of course, bombs would go astray and so we needed to head to whatever structure could double as a shelter.

However, shells fired from the Allied navy's destroyers were more frightening than bombs because when the shells hit their targets, we had no warning; no time to seek cover. The explosion of those shells was always a harrowing shock. They were so unexpected that they made us all feel particularly vulnerable. Over time, we figured out the schedule of the attacks — usually one in the morning and one before dusk. The shells from ships, however, were on no discernible time table.

During World War II, Ancona was initially not as strategically important to the Allies' plans as the beaches of Sicily or Salerno, nor as famous as the landing at Anzio Beach. As a port and a city that supported ship building of various kinds, Ancona became a target for the Allies and a position for the Axis powers to defend. In fact, significant fighting around Ancona did not begin until 1944. That is when the Allies decided they had sufficient resources to attack Hitler's Gothic Line, a defensive position in northern Italy, set up with ten-mile deep fortifications that ran from La Spezia in the west to Pesaro in the east. This line of defense was about forty miles north of Ancona.

Ancona's remoteness from the Allies' invasion of southern Italy did not mean, however, that we had arrived at a peaceful spot on the Adriatic where we could wait for the welcome arrival of United States or British soldiers. We were on the right side to greet the Allies when they came, but we were also situated in the line of both sides' fire. I already knew, from my hike in the hills near the estate, that friendly fire could be aimed at unsuspecting civilians. But my family also witnessed instances of the war that made our experience in Trieste and Split seem mild in comparison.

Also, any sense of quiet and peace was frequently interrupted. Not only were explosion of bombs a constant presence in Ancona, but so was the noise of bombers that were reserving their weapons for targets north of Italy. During our stay there we were amazed to see planes flying at high altitudes over Ancona, in what looked to be formations containing hundreds of bombers. Sometimes we would actually check our count with each other — my brother Paul and I — to see if what we were observing was actually happening. These planes were constantly traveling north and on the return run south. Later in life, when I was on the inside of strategic military planning, I learned that these aircraft were part of missions to Romania, an important source of industrial goods and grain for the Nazis. Romania was key to Germany's success as a major exporter of oil. Allied operations targeted Ploiesti, the principle site of Romania's oil industry. Its largest refinery processed two million tons of petroleum a year and provided approximately 30 percent of the fuel for the German military. United States' squadrons began bombing raids on Romania as early as June 1942. Subsequently American and British pilots flew missions to bomb Bucharest, as well as the oil fields, hoping to destroy supply lines to the Eastern Front.

The most famous of the operations to destroy Romania's oil supply took place in August, 1943. Nicknamed Operation Tidal Wave, this mobilization involved 178 U.S. B29 bombers. They left Benghazi, Libya on August 1, 1943 to drop their cargo on the oil fields in Ploiesti. These are large four-engine bombers. It proved to be one of the Allies' costliest missions during the war; 660 air crewmen did not return and 55 aircraft were lost in a 24-hour period. It was the sort of operation we witnessed from the hillside outside Ancona, even as we wondered about the objectives of the aircraft.

Between the bombing of Ancona, the shellfire from ships in the Adriatic, strafing by fighter planes, and the almost constant hum of military aircraft, we felt less safe in Ancona than in Trieste. The Allies would not occupy Ancona until July 1944, well after we had departed. For us, the journey to this seaport town had been grueling. Having fled our home in Split, and then looking for shelter in Trieste, my parents were reluctant to leave Ancona after all the miles we had travelled. As bad as the conditions were, we did not know of any better place. The positive part was there were no single or mass executions and we were still alive.

CHAPTER 13

You Can't Eat Gold

Histories of World War II naturally emphasize troop movements, artillery capacities, and battles. As important as guns, bullets, bombs, ships, planes, tanks, and jeeps were, food was arguably the most important asset during the war. Without adequate rations, the people directly engaged in combat who shot the guns, pushed the buttons, and navigated the ships would not be able to fight the war.

In 1941, famines in Greece and Leningrad, as well as one in the Netherlands in 1944, were among the tragic food shortages. In Greece, an estimated 100,000 starved to death during the German occupation, not because of crop failures but rather due to a political economy that failed to deliver the available food (which was adequate even if not abundant). In Leningrad, German occupation choked supply routes that caused the deaths of 53,000 in the fall of 1941 alone. In the last stages of the war in 1944, Germany enforced an embargo against the western section of the Netherlands in response to resistance efforts. Some of the Dutch had to resort to eating their beloved tulip bulbs. Anything to sate the ferocious pain of hunger. "Ferocious" does not properly describe the experience nor does excruciating. I can attest to that.

The issue of food partly motivated the war along Europe's eastern front. Some historians speculate that Hitler's entire battle against the Soviets was for food. In 1942, the Führer himself described the war as "a battle for food, a battle for the basis of life, for the raw materials the earth offers." In fact, one of Hitler's strategies for invading Russia was to acquire arable land. He hoped to cultivate what he called a "European California," the golden state, where produce would be as abundant as the San Joaquin Valley in the United States.

At the same time, citizens in nations like America, contributed to the war effort by observing rationing policies on simple foods like sugar, meat and butter. Such sacrifice enabled the United States soldiers to be the best-fed of any national army during World War II. According to some estimates, American G.I.s consumed as many as 4,000 calories per day — eating an astonishing amount of food. What is more likely is that United States' soldiers, who were so generous with their rations, were not consuming all of those calories by themselves, but using some of the provisions to help out starving civilians and even prisoners of war. I know this to be the case because I witnessed it.

My family and I also endured the pain that accompanied food short-ages, even though Italy did not experience extreme famine during the war. Again, the war and rudimentary political order disrupted the routes for — and carriers of — food. This meant that my basic responsibility each day during the war was to go out in search of food. The easiest item to obtain from local farmers was eggs. Usually all of the Italian farmers, after hearing our plea and observing our scrawny, dirty demeanor, could spare one egg. On a good day, we received two eggs at each stop. By the end of a full day, we hoped for a supply of a dozen eggs to be consumed by the entire family.

How we would eat them was another matter. Sometimes we might boil the eggs, other times we fried them. Frequently, we would just poke a hole in one end of the egg and then suck out its liquid and slippery insides. Americans may marvel that Rocky Balboa could put a raw egg in his beer and then gulp the entire drink down. I had no problem eating a raw egg, even without any assistance from beer. I guess we washed those eggshells before eating. But because the hunger for me was worse than any of the bombings that surrounded us, I didn't really care about the condition of those eggs. Sometimes the pangs of hunger were so intense that I could not sleep. On nights when I could not sleep, I wished for a return to those meals at my grandparents' formal dining room where I had turned my nose up at spinach and local fish. I also remember thinking that hunger is worse than death.

When we lived on the estate outside Ancona we were fortunate to be around farmers who raised hogs. I had not seen a pig butchered before. But my brother and I actually helped the farmers shove the animal up on to the table at which point the farmer stuck a knife in the pig's throat to let the blood pour out. The sights and smells, very different from what I knew in Split, were certainly strange. But the conditions of war made those scenes of slaughter less distasteful. And since farmers were usually willing to sell us some of the meat, my brother and I knew that as grisly as the procedure was, it would put food on our dinner table.

But there were times in Italy when food was so scarce that we were reduced to eating grass. Italy has a plant that was technically a grass but resembles spinach. When we could not find eggs or buy meat, we resorted to the foliage that was growing around us. It tasted awful. At one point when we were living in a village near Feltre in northern Italy, we were forced to take lodgings at a small hotel in the town so that we could have something to eat. The cook in the kitchen would prepare corn mush that they spread out on a common table from which lodgers would scoop up their breakfast, lunch, and dinner. The mush was the only item on the menu, at least most of the time. Sometimes if we were lucky, the chefs would cook up a batch of sparrows or pigeons. For me the taste did not matter. It was the first meat I had eaten for several months. To this day I am surprised that I never became overweight as an adult since food was such a precious commodity in Italy. Somehow I managed to avoid compensating for those years of hunger by overeating.

Of course, we still had our gold coins. Yet while it is true that money does not grow on trees, it is equally true that gold coins are useless if no fruit is growing on the branches.

CHAPTER 14

A Narrow Escape

My sister, Deana, is eight years older than I and her experience of our escape from Croatia and life in Italy was much different from mine, although I did not understand this at the time. As the oldest child in the family, and almost sixteen when we left Split, Deana was involved in my parents' discussions about where to live, how to travel there, what routes or places might be safe, and even where we might live, if and when, the war ended. She was also closer to adulthood than any of the four children when we left for Trieste. The war disrupted her plans for her life much more than my other sister, Gordana, my brother Paul, or me.

The war was also much more threatening to her than anyone else in the family. Of course, the bombings, the possibility of imprisonment, hunger, and filth, affected all of us in equal proportions, though the younger we were, the less our expectations had been set and the more we might be able to roll with the punches. As far as disruptions, of course, my parents suffered the most. Their settled life was gone. Still, as an older adolescent and budding young woman, Deana faced circumstances that none of us experienced directly the way that she did.

One night during our stay in Ancona, we were startled by pounding on the front door of the Villa Luxardo. We could hear Italian spoken by those knocking, which was not unusual, but we also detected German.

My parents sent us children upstairs and then went to see who was at the door.

When they looked through the window, they discovered Italian and German soldiers. My parents had their papers ready, and hoped that the official permits they had purchased in Trieste would enable the family to navigate this threatening situation. But the soldiers, as we could hear from upstairs, were not interested in our papers. At the time I could not fully comprehend German but we had native fluency in Italian. We could now speak Italian flawlessly, even without an accent, so that we could avoid detection as "foreigners." What we figured out by eavesdropping was that the soldiers were looking for young girls. It did not take detective skills to figure out their intentions. Deana was an obvious target for sexual designs.

My siblings and I sprang into action. We went to a window on the first story of the villa toward the back of the building and away from the truck that had brought the soldiers to our residence. We found a window was above a spot of ground that could easily accommodate my sister if she could climb down the outside wall of the house. And then we needed to find bedding that could double as a kind of rope. The blankets from one of our beds would do. We managed to tie sheets and blankets together, though none of us were really proficient at such a procedure. We finally lowered the bedding over the window sill and saw that it was long enough for Deana to reach the ground safely.

My brother Paul and I held on to one end of the sheets and Gordana helped Deana navigate the window while also holding on to the blankets. Meanwhile, we could hear the soldiers still talking to our parents, and they seemed to be becoming more agitated and insisted on exploring the house. These several minutes of suspense seemed to go by in slow motion. But by the time the soldiers finally climbed the stairs to see who else was inside, Deana had climbed down the side of the villa and had disappeared into the nearby woods. It was pitch black. Without light in the backyard, she would need to tread carefully. The darkness also meant that she was reasonably safe once she got away from the house and started for the trees.

The soldiers did not stay much longer once they saw that my parents had only three youngsters with them. They also did not discover our suitcase with gold coins. My father had earlier found an easily distinguishable tree where he dug a hole and buried the gold, fearing encounters like this one. But we were reluctant to retrieve Deana for a long time. When she finally rejoined us at the villa, we were all shaken but Deana was noticeably upset and only the persistent efforts of my parents consoled her.

Sexual violence was as much a part of World War II as the usual forms of armed conflict. When Germany invaded Poland, the Nazi soldiers raped Polish women in numbers impossible to calculate. The Soviet Army was also guilty of particularly brutal treatment of German women at Nemmersdorf during the last months of the war. None of the armies was immune from this enormity but I never heard of such action involving American troops. Armed aggression has gone hand in hand with sexual violence throughout the history of war. Only in 1949 did Article 27 of the Fourth Geneva Convention of 1949 make rape a war crime. It stated that "women shall be protected against any attack on their honor, in particular against rape, enforced prostitution, or any form of indecent assault." Even then, this legislation regarded rape more as a crime against a women's honor than a crime of violence.

However the authorities might have classified the intentions of the soldiers who showed up at the villa during that scary night in Ancona, we did not need a lesson in international law to know what was in store for our sister. And even though we were crafty enough to help Deana elude those soldiers, we could not prevent the scars that she would carry the rest of her life.

CHAPTER 15

Odd Bedfellows

Between the bombings, strafing, and visits from soldiers, Ancona was becoming less and less safe a place to hide. Again, alternatives were not at all obvious. In hindsight, which was a perspective not available to my parents, the decision to try to head for the Allied forces in central Italy was filled with danger in the short run. Our long-term safety would be with British and American soldiers. But until they could take control of Italy, places like Ancona would be a site of open and constant armed conflict, hardly a secure harbor in which to wait for friendly forces. Invading Anzio and Rome was an attractive approach for the Allies since these cities were defended by Italian forces. The Allies did not want to engage the Germans in Italy. In fact, the German military was not a forceful presence in Italy until after Mussolini's fall from power and General Pietro Badoglio and King Victor Emmanuel III signed a secret pact in September 1943 with the Allies.

Not until the end of the summer in 1944, would Ancona be safely on the south side of the Italian front. Operation Olive was a major offensive by British and American divisions that were designed to pinch German fortifications in the Apennine Mountains in central Italy. The plan was for British forces to attack from the east along the Adriatic coast, and the Americans from the south. Winston Churchill believed that by opening up the German "underbelly" in Italy, the Allies would have access to Austria and Hungary, be able to attack the Germans from the south in northern Europe, and prevent the Soviet forces from commandeering parts of central Europe.

To make Operation Olive possible, the Allies needed to control Ancona. The Battle of Ancona, which took place in July, 1944, was the scene of Poland's greatest success during the war. The Polish Second Corps had joined with British forces by 1944 and the Polish soldiers were responsible for capturing Ancona. Under General Wladyslaw Anders the Second Corps attacked Ancona on July 17, 1944, and controlled the city by the following day. After Ancona, the Polish soldiers joined the British Eighth Army to participate in Operation Olive.

Fortunately, we were long gone from Ancona before these efforts to take Italy away from the Germans. But those battles were an indication of the kind of danger we faced by traveling to the south in order to find a place occupied by the Allies. If we could have approached the south of Italy by sea — an impossibility because of all the war ships in the Adriatic — we might have been able to land on the other side of the fighting and enjoy some refuge. But since we could only approach the south by land, we could not avoid the fighting. If we had stayed in Ancona, my brother and I would likely have quadrupled our count of bombings in the area.

My parents sensed the danger and even though the estate where we stayed was outside town, we were vulnerable. Soldiers in the surrounding area could easily spot the edifice, and fighter pilots could also select the villa as an easy target. After all, if they could see me while hiking in the hills of Ancona, they could readily detect a villa. For some unknown reason, only one bomb came close to the estate. I remember this because I was knocked off my feet and came close to getting killed. For as long as we remained in Ancona, then, we were forced to live in the barn of the estate. My parents decided we would take refuge with the cows and other livestock in the estate's out buildings. Heating the villa turned out to be an impossible task.

Staying warm demanded resourcefulness. We used the cows to our advantage. One technique was obvious enough — to sleep with them. At night I curled up with those huge animals. I never feared that they might roll over on me, which they did not; why, I don't know. The heat they threw off was just what we needed. Some nights I actually became hot and needed to create a little space between my cow and me. The odor was another reason to move away from those good natured but awful smelling creatures.

A second technique for taking advantage of the cows was to use their waste to plug holes in the barn's walls and doors. This was a stroke of my engineering genius. I don't know why the rest of the family didn't like the idea. It worked. Now instead of howling and freezing wind, the barn had no holes and we could enjoy the warmth provided by the farm animals. Despite the danger of remaining in the villa, my sisters, Deana and Gordana, could not come to terms with living in a barn with livestock. They returned to the cold and drafty villa.

In a year, we had gone from the comfort of Split's upper class to having cows as our stall mates and a diet almost as meager as theirs. But as bad as our circumstances were, what mattered most was that we were alive. We were even convinced that we would survive these hardships because God was looking out for us. They say that there are no atheists in a foxhole. The same truth applies when in a combat zone or living in a barn.

CHAPTER 16

Leaving Italy

B y the spring of 1943, we knew we could not stay in Ancona. Doing nothing was not an option. Remaining in Italy seemed like even less of an option. Everywhere we went we faced bombings, shelling, famine, and troop movements with the prospect of armed conflict. It is easy now to understand how the best military plans and the most accomplished war technologies cannot prevent civilian casualties. Too much collateral damage occurs, and if you happen to be close enough to the scene of a battle, you become part of that damage.

So my parents determined to try to leave Italy altogether. The most appealing and closest spot for us was Switzerland, just northwest of Italy, and on the surface, a neutral country — though later revelations showed how such neutrality could work to the Axis powers' advantage. Once my parents decided to head north, the next question was how to cross the border into the nation (famous for banks, watches, and chocolate), that was not friendly.

My father hired the driver of a local public bus, one of those old vehicles with narrow tires that could hold twenty passengers at most, with seats on the roof. Gas was completely unavailable because of the war, at least the kind made from petroleum. But forms of gas existed and once again Italy's livestock came to the rescue. The locals had devised a way to create methane gas by boiling the manure of cows and humans and collecting the resulting fumes in cans. This was the fuel that would supply the energy we needed for our trip. It was called metano. Of course, we hardly required much space in the luggage compartment. We traveled light — only two small suitcases for the entire family, and one was still holding those precious gold coins.

The most direct route to Switzerland would have been along the Adriatic coast and then inland to Bolognia, followed by a direct line to Milano and Varese, which is near the Swiss border. Those towns would later become part of our itinerary, but for this trip when we reached Bolognia, our driver took a right turn to almost due north, a route that took us eventually on this trip to Feltre, a mountain town in the northern Italian province of Belluno.

When we went through Bolognia, we also saw further evidence of the Allies' efforts to subdue the Germans' control of northern Italy. From our bus we could see many bombers flying in the direction we were headed, and we heard that Bolognia was the target for many of these raids. Bolognia was a transportation hub for central Italy, the intersection of several major truck and rail arteries. Because of the bombings, we had to stop along the road, south of the city because civilians were not permitted to go into or through the city during the attacks. When we finally gained permission to enter the city, we saw a desolate place. Many buildings had been reduced to rubble. We did not see a single living human being. The remains of dead were strewn along the sides of the roads. Those still alive were in hiding. It was truly a ghost town in ruins.

After passing through the city, which took over one hour, we needed to navigate was the River Po, a tributary that runs from Monviso in the Cottian Alps, eastward across northern Italy to the Adriatic Sea near Venice. We approached the river near the town of Occhiobello at a place where no usable bridges offered access to the other side. Most of the passengers, myself and my family, had to get out of the bus in order to cross the river on foot. The bus driver drove the vehicle through the river but did not want passengers to compromise his efforts. It was also a question of safety for the passengers. Because the river bottom was uneven, and the resting place for big rocks, the bus could easily tip over. If passengers hit their heads or got caught in the vehicle, they could drown. Fortunately, it was summer and so at least the air temperature was warm even if the water was not. We zigzagged through the river, looking for stones or other places shallow enough to keep us from becoming completely soaked but to no avail. We dried out by sitting in that bus on our way to the northern hills of Italy. And if I thought I had it rough, imagine my father who had to carry the suitcase partially filled with gold, trying to lift the luggage above the water while also looking for the best route for his family. When we returned to the bus, my mother resumed her authoritative status and gave the driver a steady stream of directions and commands, and a small gold coin earning her the nickname "Dona Spada" (Iron Lady).

We still had a day's journey ahead of us. By the time we arrived in Feltre we were almost back to where we had started. Feltre is east and north of Trieste by about 100 miles. If we had simply headed for Switzerland from our first Italian destination, we could have avoided all those bombings and our wade through the River Po. But hindsight is always 20/20. Wherever we looked from our location in Europe, we saw danger. To stay alive and out of concentration camps was our paramount objective. Unfortunately, logical planning was impossible since we did not have all the information, not even a map. We were literally in God's hands.

CHAPTER 17

Battling with Nature

The place where our bus ride ended was Feltre. It was close to Switzerland. We had heard that the roads to Austria were not monitored but that access to Switzerland was. Even so, from a town in northern Italy, we were within striking distance of an exit from Italy.

Feltre was a small town in the region of Veneto, and like most of this part of Europe, rich in history. The classical author, Pliny, described the town in his accounts of the Roman Empire as a place of imperial administration. Since the first century B.C., the Empire had categorized Feltre in the second-highest class of imperial cities, which was not the best deal for residents since it gave them the responsibilities of Roman citizenship (serving in the military and paying taxes) without the rights (such as voting). After the fall of the Roman Empire, the Lombards controlled the area, and in the fourteenth century Feltre became part of the Holy Roman Empire under the reign of Charles IV. During this era, the town witnessed the construction of many edifices that continue to attract visitors, such as the city's imperial walls and gate, a cathedral dedicated to St. Peter, and a Town Hall built in the Palladian style.

Although Feltre was sufficiently accessible to attract the attention of emperors, both ancient and medieval, its location near the Dolomite Mountains on the Stizzon River and its alpine-like climate, prevented larger political or commercial development. The relative isolation of

Feltre was also responsible for the modicum of security we enjoyed when we disembarked from the bus. At the time of our arrival in 1943 the heaviest fighting had not reached the Veneto area. Even by the close of the war in the spring of 1945 — by which time we had left for Viggiu — Feltre remained untouched by the war's destruction, though the Italian front came much closer. Because the Allied forces were heading both to the northwest for France and to the east for the Balkans, the area we chose as our third major stop in Italy on the way toward freedom (we hoped) was about as safe as we could have found in the entire Italian nation.

But as secure as Feltre was, it was still subject to the forces of nature, about which we had not been concerned but did experience with a vengeance. My brother and I shared a room to ourselves. One night, while enjoying the quiet of our remote location, we awoke with a start to an entirely new kind of rumbling and crashing. An earthquake had begun and our whole room seemed to be bouncing up and down. Because pieces of the ceiling were falling down, Paul and I hid underneath our beds. From that vantage, we could hear the screams of people who needed help and the pounding of others running along the corridor to escape the deteriorating walls and ceilings. It was chaotic. I thought to myself, what's next?

When the quake stopped, we discovered that several occupants had been killed by the earthquake's destruction. We also learned that the hotel was no longer habitable. Despite the conditions of war and its hostilities, the Italian authorities commissioned soldiers to set up tents for Feltre's residents who now needed shelter. At first this proved to be a tolerable situation. For two days or so the weather was pleasant and the tents seemed adequate to our short-term needs. But when the rain came, this makeshift provision turned deplorable. The conditions were uninhabitable even to people who had shared living space with barnyard animals. Everything we had, plus the tent itself, was soaked. It was dreary, cold, and untenable. We lasted only two more weeks in those tents, before once again deciding that we must find better space. Asking for a place to protect us from bombings was one thing. But was shelter from weather too much to ask? We did not want this to be the end.

But before we could leave Feltre the war would visit us in a completely unexpected way.

CHAPTER 18

My First Act of Military Intelligence

E ven after my encounter with the United States fighter pilot on the
hills outside Ancona (periodically I still pray that he survived the
war), I continued to roam the hillsides wherever we happened to settle.
Feltre was no different, except for the downpour during our days in the
soaked tents. Even during war, life goes on. And for a boy of 12, staying inside was taxing. So out I went, usually with my brother Paul, to
explore the town, its people, and its activities.

During one of these outings, I heard a piece of gossip — Hitler was
coming to Feltre to meet and confer with Mussolini. Thanks to conversations among the townspeople — security was hardly tight — we knew
about the planned meeting two days before it took place.

Little did I know the reasons for the conference but we soon learned
the grave circumstances that had forced this meeting. Since February,
Mussolini's hold on the reins of power within Italy were growing very
weak. The Italian Army returned from the Greek campaign resolved to
end Mussolini's rule. The soldiers deployed in the Italian Alps let it be
known that they were always more loyal to the old king than to Il Duce.
The Italian people were resentful of the German presence throughout
the country. Meanwhile, in February of 1943, Mussolini dismissed his
cabinet and chief advisors, calling them a collection of malcontents.
He had nowhere to turn for loyal Fascists. Mussolini could get rid of

whomever he wanted, but he was in a war and needed loyal officers, soldiers, and citizens who would support his commitments to the Axis and his policies within Italy.

Because Mussolini had lost support among some of his cabinet, military, and the Italian people, he wanted to extract his armed forces from deployments outside the country and return them to southern Italy to defend against the Allies' expected invasion. For this reason, he was able to summon the Führer to a meeting in Feltre for the purpose of gaining German reinforcements to defend Italy, and securing orders to return Italian forces home from the Russian front. But making demands on Hitler was a lot easier said than done.

The Nazi leader and his Italian conspirator met on July 19, 1943 only a few weeks after we arrived. They chose to conduct their talks first on the train that brought him to Villa Gaggia, the palatial summer home of one of the former senators from the region. (Today it has been restored and is a working inn.) Already by this date, the Allies had scored a major victory in North Africa, and only ten days before Mussolini's visit to Feltre, American forces had landed at Anzio and were moving towards Ancona and Rome. Mussolini knew that Italy's days were numbered. According to the memoirs of those present, Il Duce was no match for Hitler who hectored Mussolini for three hours before coming up for air and lunch. Of course, these reports are questionable because no one else was in the room. But I can tell you that I was some 30 meters from the train and nobody was concerned with a kid, but I listened. The upshot of the meeting, however, was Hitler's expression of willingness to send German reinforcements to Italy if Mussolini would hand over command of his army to the German General Staff.

Mussolini left Feltre a defeated man. Back in Rome he called his Grand Council, one of his own political devices, to establish his rule over Italy. But now this body no longer gave him their support. On July 24, they voted to dismiss Il Duce from power and return the government to the King. A stubborn man, Mussolini viewed the council as merely an advisory body. When he showed up the next day at his office after their vote, the king, Victor Emmanuel III, had Mussolini arrested.

As good as the news of the dictator's ouster was to us, it also posed several problems. First, it did not really change the aims of the Allies or Hitler's need for Italy. Warfare in Italy would not subside any time soon and we would need to choose our path carefully. That was in the long run. In the short run, the presence of more German soldiers throughout Italy was not welcome news, especially given the flimsiness of our papers and our true homeland. Of even more immediate concern to my parents was what this meeting might do to this strategic area of Feltre. They were sure that the visit of the two Axis leaders would draw the attention of the Allies and send more bombings in our direction. This did not happen.

CHAPTER 19

Finding a Dentist

By the summer of 1943, my family and I had made our way to Maggio, a quaint Italian village in the Italian Alps, where we stayed in a small hotel. Since leaving Split eighteen months earlier, we had traveled some 800 miles between Trieste in the northeast, Ancona on the east coast, and now northern Italy near the border of Switzerland.

One reason for leaving Feltre was still to find a route into Switzerland. Although the Swiss did not take sides formally during the war, we heard stories that demonstrated Switzerland was hardly neutral. Italian and German soldiers could pass freely across the Swiss border; in fact, after the war, German soldiers found Switzerland to be a safe harbor while the Allies restored order in Italy. But most citizens were not so free to cross the Swiss border. Sometimes, we heard people say, people trying to enter Switzerland illegally would be shot by Swiss Border Guards. I believe this to be true but did not witness it.

If we could not enter Switzerland from the southeast (near routes to Innsbruck), then maybe we could find a friendlier route to the West, near Lake Como. So the family traveled by truck — my father once again found a driver who was willing to carry a vagabond family — to Como, stopping first at Lecco. From Lecco we went north to Maggio — a small town situated in the mountainous region of Lombardy. This village had very little to distinguish it from the surrounding villages and the landscape made it a place far from the beaten path. In other words, it was perfect for people who were hoping to get out of war's way. This village had nothing to attract the attention of princes, generals, or financiers. It was truly a quiet and peaceful village — even beautiful because untouched by war. No soldiers were coming through as part of deployments to the front, no bombing raids sent residents scurrying for shelters. The people were not interested in aiding Partisan resistance members, and no political leaders wanted to conduct negotiations there. Best of all, it was close to Switzerland if we could discover a place to cross the border.

When we arrived in Maggio, the village and surrounding region felt safe, or so it seemed when my parents decided we would remain there. The Italian army was spread out in places other than its homeland. They were still an occupying force east of the Adriatic Sea in Croatia, Serbia, and Albania. They had failed in their attempts to invade Greece but were initially successful in North Africa in 1940 where they occupied Libya and Egypt before meeting resistance from British forces. There were of course conflicts with the Italian Partisans, one of which I experienced firsthand the day recounted at the beginning of this book.

As previously stated, my brother Paul and I were used to going out on excursions to look for food for the rest of the family because hunger was still our constant painful companion with few exceptions when we occasionally stayed in a hotel. Sometimes local farmers would have extra eggs, vegetables, and even meat. I became accustomed to the sight of pigs and cows being slaughtered, while I hoped the farmer might be willing to sell us a few cuts of meat. We bartered for produce and sometimes paid in gold when necessary. Hunger was still the enemy that would not let go; it was almost constantly eating away at us. It was agony.

When I went to the dentist to find relief for my aching tooth, we soon learned how fragile safety was in remote places like Maggio mentioned in the Prologue. The sounds of gunshots and wailing, the sight of burning vehicles, dead bodies and terrorized women will do that. Of course, we later learned that our friend's mother had died along with almost fifty body guards who were responsible to protect her.

Paul and I knew enough not to stop for long. So we kept pedalling on the bikes and eventually made it to town. The ride allowed us to gain our composure. It was also enough time for me to be reminded of how much my tooth hurt.

We eventually found the dentist. I persuaded him to take a look at my mouth. But just as I sat down in his chair the town's sirens blared with warnings about a raid. Apparently, the Communists were not finished, had come to the village, and had opened fire. They were not looking for Paul and me, but they may well have been fleeing the Italian military and police who by then had responded to the assassination and were in pursuit.

Paul and I did not spare any time to find out the reason for the Partisan raid. We found our bikes and proceeded to pedal back up the mountainside to the safety of our family and their accommodations. Adrenaline was a great help up the hill and the danger enabled me to forget my toothache. When we saw the dead body of our friend's mother during our return, we pedaled even faster. This time passing the scene, the Italian Fascist soldiers, let us go through as readily as had the Partisans.

Needless to say, we returned home without any food that day. We were thankful to be alive. And for a moment, I had forgotten about my tooth and remembered the war that surrounded us and was the impetus for our exilic way of life. That night I prayed — extra long and hard.

CHAPTER 20

Closer to Safety

After the ambush of my friend's mother, Maggio became a much less peaceful place. The Italian government retaliated by conducting a full-scale search of the area, hoping to find the Partisans who were responsible for the brutality. They called it **restraliamento**. The process involved divisions of soldiers combing through the surrounding hills and farms and executing anyone suspicious. As you might imagine, the Partisans did not sit back and let the Italian soldiers find their fortifications and hiding places. They fought back and so war returned to a place where we had enjoyed a measure of tranquility. This was like the fighting that had forced us first to leave Split and then Trieste. It was not part of the war between the Axis and Allied forces as part of the global contest between tyranny and freedom but skirmishes between local factions along the typical ideological lines of contemporary Europe — Fascist, Communist, and Royalist.

With the proximity of dangerous fighting, my parents decided to relocate yet again, the sixth during our exile in Italy. The place they chose was Viggiu. Here my father knew the owner of a hotel from pre-war days. The town was about an hour's drive from Maggio, which we traveled again with the aid of a local truck driver whom my father hired for the journey. As normal as life had been in Maggio, we also knew that our fortunes could change at any moment. For that reason, my parents were still considering an exit strategy from Italy. No one knew how long the war would last, or if we would survive. Consequently, our relocation to Viggiu, in the province of Varese, another small town that had more activity than Maggio, put us even closer to the Swiss border. The chief industry for this town, nestled at the base of a mountain, was stone cutting, a line of work that had little direct bearing on a wartime economy. But again the lack of activity and remoteness of Viggiu was highly appealing to us. Aside from putting us only a few miles from the Swiss border, the town allowed us to continue living in relative tranquility.

One indication of a return to normal life was the acquisition of shoes. For most of the war to this point, I was living without shoes. This was extremely painful, especially during the winter months. But in Viggiu, I finally got shoes. These were not your typical foot gear. They were wooden and uncomfortable, and prevented me from running at full speed. Still, they retained some body heat and protected my feet from rocks, water, and glass. We usually associate wooden shoes with the Dutch. But they were also common in Switzerland and northern Italy among peasants and farmers. Today these shoes have the fashionable name of clogs.

The other sign that our life had resumed some regularity was the availability of food. Granted, we had no choice in what we ate. The only food that we could obtain cheaply and in moderate quantities was rice. For flavor we added saffron, which was also readily available. Eating rice, seasoned with saffron, day after day was monotonous, broken only by the occasional catching and cooking of sparrows. To this day, I cannot stand the taste or smell of saffron. But at the time it was wonderful. In this case, monotony was good. After all that we had experienced — especially the desperate hunger of Ancona — a regular diet, no matter how boring, was almost blissful.

In Viggiu we started to become optimistic about the end of the war. One of our neighbors in the hotel had a wireless and this gave us access to broadcasts from "Radio London." (Eventually this radio production became part of the BBC World Service, an arm of the broadcast company's reporting on developments in all parts of the world.) But Radio London was a small operation when it first started in 1932, only broadcasting in English to the European continent. By 1942, the broadcasts were in all the major European languages and Radio London became a vehicle for following the war's progress. By the time we reached Viggiu, we learned that the Germans were clearly on the defensive, clinging to a few strongholds on the Western Front and engaged in a stalemate against the Allies' advance in Italy. Although we did not know how long it would take, with the Allies' successful advance through France and the Soviets' attacks in eastern Europe, the Nazis' days were numbered.

We could not reveal our knowledge of or interest in these broadcasts openly. In fact, we always needed to meet in secret lest the authorities find the radio or — worse — take the audience away, never to be seen again. So we developed a code, both for access to the hotel and the room where the radio could be heard and to inform those not present about the day's war developments. The signal that I heard repeatedly, a sound forever etched in my memory, was three short taps followed by a pause and then one longer and louder tap. This was as close as we could come to replicating the Morse Code for the letter "V." It meant victory, of course, and it was memorably the last set of signals we would hear as we waited and hoped for the Allies' victory. This was the most welcome part of the life that we knew in Viggiu. Far more than shoes, a bathroom, clothes or food, I wanted an end to the fighting and the opportunity finally to settle and make a new home. I never doubted that we would survive and find our way to safety. This belief gave me courage that served me well in life. God was looking out for us.

CHAPTER 21

Another in a Series of Unpleasant Experiences

My Uncle Nikola — or Niko — escaped from Yugoslavia while we were in Viggiu and somehow managed to find us. Perhaps my parents were carrying on a more sophisticated form of communication than I was aware of, but I had no idea how my uncle was able to find us. We had no telephones. Postal service was non-existent. And yet he orchestrated a trip to northern Italy and found his brother, my father, and family in the remote area of the Italian Alps where we were hiding.

Mike's Uncle Nikola Novakovic, who practiced medicine and advised

He must have used contacts in the Catholic church to locate us.

His arrival was welcome news, not only to see a relative who had escaped war-torn Yugoslavia, but also because Uncle Niko was a physician. He had served briefly as an assistant to the nation's prime minister at the time of the king's assassination, thus making him a marked man to the Partisans. I looked to Niko's arrival as my last connection to my homeland. My parents and I had assumed that Uncle Vlado had been a casualty of the continuing war in Yugoslavia. As it turned out, he had managed to elude both the Axis forces and the Partisans by taking refuge in the Novakovic hometown of Knin. There the local peasants had taken him in. I am still curious and perhaps one day I will find out the circumstances.

Soon after Uncle Niko's arrival, I experienced unbearable pain in my stomach, along with the classic signs of appendicitis which included fever and vomiting. Once my uncle examined me and discovered how sensitive my stomach was, even to his touch, he concluded that I had peritonitis and that my appendix had burst. This was life-threatening. Medical facilities were distant and access to civil authorities who might help, even more

Uncle Nikola speaking on the radio

remote. My uncle knew I needed to get to a hospital immediately if I were to survive. The question was where?

The closest facility to our remote location was in Varese, a town approximately ten miles from our residence but much harder to access because of many check points along the way. The hospital there was not much more than a clinic. It was a house of few rooms, converted into a medical facility. It was the only "hospital" in the region, with one physician, two nurses, and one operating room. The doctor would have to double as a surgeon and a mortician.

The procedure itself was the least painful part of the episode even though the hospital had no general anesthesia to administer during my surgery. All the hospital staff could do to reduce the pain from the incision was to give me a series of shots that numbed my stomach. Maybe because the local anesthesia also brought relief from the intense pain of my burst appendix I did not mind being awake for the procedure. At the time this surgery seemed like an improbable addition to a series of difficulties that marked our time in Italy. But I took this surgery in stride. Because I was awake I got to hear and watch an operation, always an attraction to a boy.

If removing my appendix had been the whole of the matter, I would have simply returned to my family after a week of recuperation at the hospital. But medical conditions being what they were, the treatment after surgery proved to be even more painful than the peritonitis itself. I was given castor oil, which was almost a kiss of death. One of the nurses mistakenly administered it. This caused the infection in my stomach to be exacerbated and my life was now in grave danger. The pain returned with a vengeance. Castor oil was the last thing that I should have been given. This time I did not think I could make it but I hoped.

Because antibiotics were non-existent, the only treatment for the infection was a prolonged therapy of sulfa drugs, which were very expensive and continued to drain my father's savings. Instead of being able to recover in a few days, I was in the hospital some two months. It felt like an eternity. My parents came to visit as often as possible. But they were still in Viggiu and had no access to transportation other than walking the distance between their village and the town of Varese. Meanwhile, my uncle had to get out of the area altogether. Maybe because he helped to gain admittance for me to the hospital, word circulated that he was not truly who his papers said he was. My family's papers looked legitimate but if pressed, authorities could have given us a hard time, particularly if they knew that we came from Yugoslavia. But Niko's Yugoslavian identity put us all in peril at the time. So he left Varese and went back to Croatia with the help of contacts in the Vatican. (He died after the war in Knin.) But at the time, I was at the mercy of the hospital's "staff" all by myself.

As if appendicitis was not enough, the hospital was located next door to a facility that the Gestapo used to torture their prisoners. During the day and throughout the night I could actually hear the groans and screams of the Nazis' victims. It was sickening. Sometimes the screams and sobbing would stop but only after a shot. The person who had been pleading for mercy, had been executed. I did not understand the full significance of what went on in that building. But at the same time I knew enough to realize that my own circumstances were not as monstrous as what others were experiencing.

Such an outlook, though, was much harder to maintain when the sirens, warning of a bombing raid on Varese, sent the hospital's help away from the town for the better part of two nights. The Gestapo facility next to the hospital was likely the target of these raids. I was in no condition to leave my bed. I was very sick and weak that the only recourse the physician had was to leave me in the hospital by myself. I was still in so much pain, thanks to the infection, I actually did not think I would survive. In those days, precision bombing did not exist. The next morning I did not have any food but it didn't matter. Hunger was not going to kill me this time but the infection might. But the raid missed both the Gestapo prison and also the hospital.

For three days and two long nights, I was entirely alone in my hospital room. I could not get out of bed to use the toilet. My parents did visit one time, and brought some food and water. I was, of course, in no condition to eat. That was one of the few times during the war when I experienced genuine fear. I was completely helpless. I could do nothing to get well, and I was at the total mercy of where the bombers dropped their arsenal of explosives, as well as a hospital staff who disappeared.

The old adage has it that it is darkest before the dawn. Certainly it applied to me. It was very, very, very dark. Gradually, I began to see some light but I don't know how. After so many days that turned into weeks, I was finally able to return to my family in Viggiu. I learned how close the war was to ending. But of all the times when I might have been killed, either by Communists death squads or Croatian Fascists, Allied bombs or strafing, or German artillery, the closest I came to death was when my own body almost failed. And my brush with death came just when my family and I were closest to freedom and safety.

CHAPTER 22

Victory

Hearing the Morse code for "V" or listening to reports by Radio London about the end of the Second World War was one thing, but actually experiencing it was another. From our vantage in Viggiu, we did not have a ringside seat like the Europeans in Paris or London who gathered in public squares to celebrate Victory in Europe Day (VE Day), May 8, 1945, the day that marked the unconditional surrender of the Nazi forces to the Allies. But our observations were no less significant and likely even more poignant than the revelry of the English who gathered at Buckingham Palace to observe King George VI, Queen Elizabeth, and Winston Churchill waving to the crowds, or the French who thronged to the Champs Elysees singing the Marseilles.

The first indication that the war had changed dramatically was the procession of German soldiers who passed through Viggiu on their way across the border into Switzerland. At first, when we heard the tanks coming — and by then we knew the distinct sound of the Nazi Tiger Tanks — we feared that armed conflict was again coming our way. After all, soldiers far removed from military headquarters or official negotiations have been known to continue fighting after a formal declaration of cease-fire or surrender. But instead of looking for Partisans or Allied soldiers, and instead of setting up camp, these soldiers proceeded straight into Switzerland at a high rate of speed. Unlike the screening that many refugees experienced during the war who hoped to find shelter in Switzerland, these German soldiers moved quickly through Viggiu and vanished into the murky world of Swiss diplomacy.

Another indication of the changes afoot was the arrival of another set of tanks. This time we knew from the noise that these were not another division of Tiger Tanks. As we waited to see what would turn out to be our first sighting of the Allies during the entire war, we encountered an insignia entirely foreign to my parents and me. On these tanks was a triangle, with a green border on the outside and a patch of yellow in the middle. This was the insignia of the Sixth South African Armored Division, a unit that served in the Italian campaign under the command of the British Eighth Army. The South Africans were deeply involved in the last conflicts in northern Italy and these tanks — a unit of several dozen or so — were coming through Viggiu to make sure that the German presence had left. They did not stay long. They were very friendly and waved to the civilians but had no food or provisions to distribute to the hungry populace. After inspecting the small town's streets and seeing no signs of the Axis forces, the South Africans left almost as quickly as they arrived. There were no longer signs of the Gestapo or execution squads.

The third deployment of tanks to arrive in Viggiu in May of 1945 was the charm. A unit of British tanks arrived a day or so after the South Africans and they were a welcome sight, simply because the arrival of two consecutive Allied units meant that they were in control in our region and that the war was conforming to reports we heard on the radio. We were also grateful for these British soldiers because they brought much needed food. Granted, we were eating regularly in Viggiu, thanks to the availability of rice, but when the British came we finally enjoyed something other than our bland saffron flavored dish. My brother and I were especially keen on the candy bars that the Allies brought. We had not eaten anything sweet for almost four years. Now we enjoyed a large selection of candy that, without the supervision of my sister and mother, would have likely made us sick if we had eaten it as quickly and ravenously as we wanted.

One of the comical signs of the war's end was the change of colors outside the homes of Viggiu as these Axis and Allies tanks came through town. When the locals saw the Germans coming, they quickly flew German flags outside their homes. But then when the Allied units arrived, the residents quickly took down the German flags and replaced them with British colors. Sometimes they would also revert to the flags of their own government, the green, red, and white colors of Italy. In one day this change of national flags must have happened five times. So eager were the Italians to be on the right side that they made sure to display the correct signs of loyalty. Who could blame them — anything to have the war over and a return to peace.

More sobering was the fate that awaited the local residents who had cooperated with the Fascists during the war. The local chief of police functioned as the mayor, the only one with the power to establish order. He was a good man and did not like the Fascists. He wanted to make sure that their sympathizers knew their ideology and efforts were no longer welcome. Soon after VE Day, he rounded up the women who had collaborated with the Fascists. He then proceeded to have their heads shaved. This occurred in the town square for everyone to see. On one level, this was much better than beating or killing the women. It struck me as a humane way to inflict punishment for what the chief considered war crimes. On another level, it was a severe form of retribution because of the humiliation involved. The shaved head was also a sign to others, and a lengthy reminder to the women themselves. As long as it would take for their hair to grow back, they and others would know of their loyalties during the war. A small price to pay, in my mind, but I did not like to see the women suffer.

And to my family and me, those shaved heads were a sign that we no longer needed to maintain our secret existence. We could now think about finding a home rather than a temporary shelter away from bombings and fighting. The big question was — where is home? With God's help, we would find it and we did.

CHAPTER 23

A Milano Apartment

When the war ended, my parents had to decide what to do next. Their first decision was to leave Viggiu for the closest Italian city of significant size. Milano, only about 40 miles south of where we were living, was their choice. It was a major transportation hub, a place where the Allies soon established a presence, and an urban center that would have access to offices, consulates, and banks — agencies that we needed if we were going to leave Italy.

Although the war was over, the future of Italy was very much in question. Since 1943 the southern part, occupied by the Allies, had been governed by U.S. and British peace-keeping forces. In the north, however, where the Nazis clung to power, the Italian monarchy, back in control after Mussolini's ouster, oversaw a fragile constellation of pro-Fascist, Communist, and Republican factions. We lacked the means or time to travel as far as southern Italy where the Allies would have provided a more congenial resource for leaving Italy. For that reason, we needed to wait in Milano and hope that a government hostile to us, would not come into power.

From the start of our time there, we feared a Communist-dominated government because of strong opposition to the Fascists and the anarchy that had prevailed. At the same time, Stalin had been plotting with leaders of the Communist Party in Italy since 1943 for ways to establish a Communist government and extend Soviet influence in southern Europe. These plans did not come to fruition, partly because of conflicts among Soviet, Yugoslav, and Italian Communists over Trieste and who would be allowed to control it. In 1946, Italy conducted a referendum that became the basis for the country's status as democratic republic. Even then, however, the Communist party remained strong within the Italian Parliament.

Although we could not travel as far as the Allied controlled territory of southern Italy, we were able to meet a U.S. officer in Milano who was crucial to our finding a post-war home. During our initials in the city, my father met a colonel whom I will call "Colonel Jager," who was an American citizen. During the entire war, Colonel Jager worked within the Nazi intelligence unit and functioned as the chief for the Allies on German espionage. My father's German was very good and he immediately struck up a friendship with Colonel Jager; they shared stories about old haunts in Vienna. Having this high level American official looking out for us was a major coup. It was in fact a miracle! He became the head of Allied forces in Milano and one of the chief officers responsible for the government during the postwar months of the many transitions with Italian society. (He would eventually become a successful businessman in the United States. I later befriended his daughter, who attended Syracuse University.) In the long run, he assisted us in acquiring visas for leaving Italy. In the short run, he helped us find a home.

Thanks to Colonel Jager we enjoyed our first encounter with accommodations like those we had known in Split three years earlier. He designated a large apartment near the central square in Milano to be our residence. He also made provisions for it to be furnished. We finally had access to our own beds, a living room, kitchen and perhaps most important — a bathroom and food. For most of the war, we had not been able to bathe with any regularity. And thanks to the provisions supplied by the Allies, we also now enjoyed multiple changes of clothes. So instead of wearing the same underwear, shirt, and pants, we could don clean clothes upon our clean bodies. I am not sure any thirteen-year-old has enjoyed taking a bath as much as I did in our new home. But as homey as our new residence was, we were surrounded by reminders of the war. The area closest to our building was reduced to rubble.

One of the most memorable aspects of that apartment was the front door. The rooms had actually been used by S.S. officers during the war, and the apartment doubled as their headquarters. That explained the thick, metal door at the apartment's entrance, obviously designed to withstand attacks.

We had come a long way since we left Split even though we had been confined to travel within northern Italy. When we set out, we were hoping to find friendly soldiers who would provide the security we needed to escape the ravages of war. As it turned out, we never found those soldiers until after the fighting had ceased and the armistice was signed. The safety we hoped to find came from our own craftiness and perseverance. Still, making friends with Colonel Jager was well-timed. As much as we had been able to elude the direct assault of bombs and the confinement of prison or concentration camps, we would need official help if we were ever to escape Europe.

CHAPTER 24

The Final Fall of Mussolini

O nce we established our presence in Milano and I fully recovered from surgery and the subsequent infection, I returned to my old ways of exploration. Milano was a place that offered many outlets for a boy's escapades. But three years of war and recent experiences in Maggio and Viggiu had matured me. The old adventures of tormenting soldiers were no longer necessary. My brother and I still had lots of rambunctious energy, but we were not interested in stirring up trouble. We wanted to help because experienced enough war.

Milano was one of Italy's most important cities. It became part of the Roman Empire in the third century BC, and five hundred years later, under Diocletian, became the capital of the Western half of the Roman Empire, with Constantinople functioning as the center of administrative life for the Eastern half. When Emperor Constantine in 313 decreed that Christians should no longer be persecuted but should instead enjoy freedom to practice their faith, one of the great turning points in the history of religious tolerance, the emperor signed this treaty — the Edict of Milan — in Milano. Because of its geography and political importance, Milano was a transportation hub throughout its history. It emerged in the twentieth century as one of the largest commercial and population centers in southern Europe. But before our arrival, Milano had experienced much warfare, some of the most violent in 1945. Although Italy was no longer fighting on Germany's side after 1943, the German occupation of northern Italy meant that Milano was a vital link in the Nazi efforts to maintain control and to defeat the Allies' campaign headed north into central Europe. Consequently, the city endured severe bombing in 1944 and the main target was Milano's main railway station. Contributing to the ground attacks on Milano, was the deployment of Partisan resistance forces against the German military and administrative units. In fact, when the war finally ended, the Germans lost control of Milano, not because of the U.S. First Armored Division, which was fast approaching the city in the spring of 1945, but because of the Italian resistance.

As I explored the city, I saw the devastating effects of the bombings. One of the most ghoulish scenes was the sight of Mussolini at the Piazza Loreto. Milano had been the place of Il Duce's first prominence as an Italian ruler. In 1919 he organized the Blackshirts, the Italian Fascist organization, in Milano and the city was the base for his initial operations. In 1922 the Fascists March on Rome started in Milano. A little over two decades later Milano also witnessed the dictator's ultimate downfall. Once he fell from power in 1943, Mussolini was arrested by the new Italian government, led by King Victor Emmanuel and Prime Minister Pietro Badoglio. But once Badoglio signed a pact with the Allies and declared war on the Nazis, the Germans rescued Mussolini and forced him to create another Fascist government in Italy. There was constant confusion. Chaos prevailed.

Il Duce again found favor with the Germans who were planning to help him escape the Allied forces. He was on a German convoy, headed for Switzerland when the Partisans caught up with him and his associates. At Dongo, a town very near Maggio within a mile of the Swiss border, the Partisans found the convoy, searched the trucks, and identified Mussolini, who was wearing a German enlisted man's coat over his general's pants. He was soon reunited with his mistress, Clara Petacci. The council of Partisan leaders issued an order to execute Mussolini, his girlfriend, and some fifteen other Fascists.

The Partisans did more than execute the dictator. They proceeded to beat Il Duce brutally and then shot him several times including once below his groin. They also executed his mistress. On April 29, 1945, the Partisans took Mussolini's body, along with the other high level executed Fascists, to the Piazza Loreto in Milano, where they hung his body, still wearing underwear and pants, upside down on meat hooks from the rafters of an Esso (yes, Esso) gas station. The dictator's face was disfigured and one side of his head looked as if it had almost been crushed. Blood on his shirt near his stomach revealed another bullet wound. But his captors clearly had spent most of their time bludgeoning Mussolini's body. His arms and hands dangled helplessly.

Benito Mussolini and Claretta Petacci, his mistress. They were shot and then hung on April 29, 1945

When I arrived at the plaza, the people were just watching, probably because of superstitions which ran deep in the Italian people and prevented tampering with the dead. I also noticed that some were hosing the bodies down, hoping to preserve the spectacle and prevent decomposition of the body for as long as possible. By the time I arrived, Mussolini's body had been there for some three days.

Part of the reason for allowing this kind of public humiliation was to discourage any further fighting by the Fascists. It was also retaliation, I later learned, for the hanging of Partisans at this same place by the Fascist government. The citizens of Milano yelled insults at the Italian dictator. It was a grim lesson about Italian politics; although the war had involved most of the world, it also tapped into the deep conflicts among the Italian people.

When I returned home, I was naturally excited by what I had seen and told my parents innocently enough. Since so many people had been in the square observing the bodies, and I had seen so many other dead bodies during the course of the war, I hardly thought that I was guilty of misconduct. But my parents were not happy with me. They said I shouldn't have gone to the plaza. When I asked why, the best they could do was to comment on the lack of dignity in such a public display. Desecrating the defeated and the dead was not something of which they approved. I was glad it was over. That night I must have repeated The Lord's Prayer in Italian over 100 times.

CHAPTER 25

Underage Military Intelligence

I was not aware of it at the time, but I received my first training in military intelligence during our time in Milano. I am not sure how much my parents knew about this, but they were aware that Paul and I were spending a lot of time with the Allies' military police in Milano. They figured that military police would be even better at monitoring young boys than parents. They could not help but know that my brother and I were cooperating with the British and Americans because we eventually were wearing British and American military uniforms.

Paul and I had pretty much free reign to explore the city. We had grown up during the war — in many ways we didn't really have a childhood. So my parents gave us lots of room to go out to different parts of the city on our own. The trams were running — amazing since so much of the city had been destroyed — and we could hop on one for free and go almost anywhere we wanted. On one stop, we went to the Milano zoo, one of the better facilities in pre-war Europe. It is amazing that there *was* a zoo since so much of the city was destroyed. We will never forget the house that was home to the hippopotamuses. It was a small building and the crowds were pressed in close to the bars separating patrons from the animals the day Paul and I visited. I was fascinated by the huge hippos — two of them. I had never seen any animals so large — not even the cows in Ancona — and these animals were completely foreign to Europe. At one point the scene took a turn for the worse that also turned out to be funny to an adolescent. One of the hippos turned its backside to the people, crowded into this small building, and projectilely released its bowels and bladder. Everyone got hit by the waste, even though we tried to evacuate as quickly as possible. I never ran as fast from bombs as I did from that hippo's spray. But it was exhilarating to two boys, all in the course of a day in Milano.

Another stop we made was at the headquarters of the British military police. Paul and I saw the signs, wondered if they might have some food, and decided to drop in. We struck up a conversation with the guards and officers and even though our English was not perfect, they recognized that Paul and I spoke native Italian, which could be of great help to them.

We did not need to be lured into assisting them. They asked if we wanted to take a ride in one of their jeeps. Of course, we wanted to. After the ride through one of Milano's neighborhoods, the British officers gained even more of our confidence by offering us chocolates and food that we could take back to our family. So for the next few weeks, as long as the British were in Milano, my brother and I went every day to the military police headquarters and assisted their efforts to restore order in Milano. The work involved translating their instructions and orders to the native population. I learned quickly how to give orders.

Soon the American military police took over for the British, and the Yanks continued to use our language skills even more. The arrival of the Americans was like manna from heaven. My brother and my whole family regarded the American G.I.s as an absolute force for good, and they were the ones we had been looking for during the entire war. The American military police also provided us with uniforms. They continued to let us have as much food as we

Roof of American Military Police Building, Milano

wanted, both for us during the day and to take home to our family at the apartment. And they were unintentionally responsible for letting us hear music for the first time in four years. The G.I.s kept the bars and night clubs open, several of which were near our apartment even though the entire area was devastated. The sounds orchestrated in those wasteland settings were wonderful music to our famished ears.

The Americans even used us when they went out on raids of various kinds. One of the greatest difficulties the Americans faced was the loss of personal property to Italian thieves. Because Milano was a transportation center, when the trains began to run again, it became the place where most U.S. soldiers serving in Italy embarked either for home or another base of operation in post-war Europe. The trucks transporting the soldiers were filled with bags of personal effects — an easy target for locals who were quick to spot items they could either use themselves or sell on the black market.

Paul and I assisted the American military police's efforts to deter the stealing. Sometimes we simply translated their warnings to the locals, instructing them that if they continued to steal they would be punished. Other times we actually went on raids to round up the thieves. I myself chased and caught several Italian thieves. I didn't suffer because of my youth, and with my speed I could usually catch anyone. Fighting was another matter. The United States soldiers tried to teach me how to box, mainly as a form of amusement. I went through some of the informal lessons and also sparred with a young soldier, a kid not much older than I, from Kentucky, and about my size. He pummeled me the first several bouts, but once I got the knack of fighting, I actually knocked him out. It was the last time he wanted to fight me. I became adept at helping the M.P.s catch the Italian thieves. After capturing and arresting them, we took them ten or

*Mike (left) and Paul
in U.S. uniforms*

so miles outside of town and dropped them off. The thieves would then have to walk all the way back into Milano. It was certainly not a harsh punishment, but effective.

GI who befriended us

We developed a very good working rapport with the Americans and in full uniforms we were indistinguishable from them. They treated us well, so much so that you could say they adopted us. And we clearly looked up to them because they were decent, good-hearted, and even virtuous young men. One of the men, Sergeant Redmond, became a friend with whom we corresponded after he returned to the United States. He went back to his home in Roanoke, Virginia, and became a school teacher and then a principal. Paul, as an adult, visited Redmond in Virginia.

Aside from the human bonds we were forming, one of my favorite experiences while working with the Americans was chewing gum. When I received my first stick of gum I thought it was a precious commodity and would only chew a quarter of a stick at a time. I had never had chewing gum before. For the entire war we did not have any of the small pleasures to which the Allies' soldiers were exposing us. I soon figured out, though, that chewing gum was plentiful and free, so it was okay to chew an entire stick at a time. The abundance did not diminish my enjoyment, however. I may have had more food, candy, and clothing while growing up in Split, but by 1945, that was a distant memory.

What I remember most were the desperate times and the agony of hunger and the indescribable conditions under which we lived throughout our sojourn in Italy. Now, work with the Americans opened up opportunities that I could not have imagined only a few months earlier. Our unlikely work with the military police made a lasting impression. It eventually determined the course of my working career and affected the lives of my family — all for the good.

CHAPTER 26

Citizens of Rome

As rewarding as my work with the American soldiers was, as much as we enjoyed the good will and assistance of Colonel Jager, as comfortable as our apartment was, and as easy as it was to find food and treats, we could not stay in Milano. We were still stateless. Our original Italian papers were worthless now that Mussolini's government was no longer in power. Returning to Yugoslavia was not an option. Tito's rule in our old country was no place for people like my father who came from Royalist background and had brothers in the Yugoslav Royal Army and priests in the Serbian Orthodox Church. Clearly, Tito followed policies designed not to tolerate the various ethnicities and nationalities of post-war Yugoslavia. In fact, my father's politics were not welcome. He was a marked man in Tito's Yugoslavia. A paper issued by Tito's government in Kotor, in the Yugoslavian region of Montenegro, specified that my father was "an enemy of the state" and should be "executed on sight."

If executive orders like this were not enough to make us fear the rule of Communism, politics in post-war Milano were. Because of the instability of the Italian political system, many natives feared a Communist takeover. In Milano, the Communist party had a vociferous if not a large following. In the square over which our apartment looked, we regularly saw mass demonstrations by the Communists. They would assemble there, carrying flags that bore the hammer and sickle, the symbol of international Communism, and singing their songs of Communist solidarity. The local Italian authorities in the city, however, were adamantly opposed to Communism and took strong but effective measures to suppress them.

One day during the Communist violent protest that filled the square adjacent to our quarters, we saw many jeeps, obtained by Milano's officials, drive straight into the mass of people. Not only did the drivers not try to avoid any of the protesters, but on the sides of the jeep were Italian police who wielded large bars, maybe six feet long. They would swing these bars at anyone in the square they could reach. The assaults on the demonstrators cleared twenty-foot swaths in the square, leaving the injured and, in few cases, the dead. This was heavy handed and showed the kind of residual effect from the war and that it was still a part of European politics. But these methods also eliminated many of the mass protests. From then on, the Communists would have to use other tactics.

As a family we could not face a possible internal war and made the decision to leave Italy. Colonel Jager was very helpful and encouraging, so we first applied for visas to the United States. But the U.S. officials in Milano only received our application. We learned that we would need to wait five years before being able to go to America. We next applied to South Africa, which would have taken us almost immediately but my sister, Deana, had strong reservations about emigrating there, mainly because of low standards of living. Our sights were really set on the United States rather than on British outposts whether in Africa or Australia. For the time being, this left South America as the most likely immediate destination. Of course, many Nazis and Fascists were following the "Ratlines," the escape routes established secretly for soldiers and even war criminals, to Argentina. The involvement of the Vatican in these relocation efforts has generated bad publicity for the Roman Catholic curia. Bishop Alois Hudal, rector of the Pontificio Istituto

Teutonico di Santa Maria dell'Anima in Rome, a seminary for Austrian and German priests, was one Roman official who helped secure safe passage for many ex-Nazis, some of whom would have been tried as war criminals. They also helped us and many others. Through Colonel Jager's help, as well as my Uncle Niko, who was well connected to Serbian Orthodox priests, Roman Catholic officials were willing to issue visas to my family to gain legal permission for migrating to South America.

But we were not headed for Argentina like many of the Nazis and Fascists. Instead, our visas were supposed to take us to Paraguay. The route would be from Genoa by way of Buenos Aires to Asuncion. My father was not at all content with a plan that would take us to Paraguay, a country that was undergoing the same sort of conflict that Yugoslavia had experienced prior to the invasion of the Germans and Italians. (A civil war eventually engulfed Paraguay in 1947 and political stability would not emerge until 1954 with the rule of the dictator, Alfredo Stroessner.)

When we said goodbye to our comfortable Milano apartment and took the train for Genoa to board a ship for Buenos Aires, we were about to embark again on a voyage with an uncertain final destination. Just as we had left Split in 1942 for the alleged purpose of enjoying a picnic in Pula, so we left Milano three years later with the legally stated purpose of emigrating to Paraguay. But just as we had left Split not knowing where we would wind up after reaching Trieste, so we left Italy for Buenos Aires hoping eventually to find our way to the United States. Having endured the uncertainties and depravations of the war, the voyage to South America did not seem different from what we had experienced. At least the war was over and our papers were legitimate.

CHAPTER 27

Under the Radar

World War II introduced the legal distinction between a refugee and an immigrant. This was an understandable development; since the end of the war, an unprecedented dispersion of people took place throughout Europe and even around the world. One solution to the problem of displaced persons that the American, British, and Russian authorities arrived at during the Potsdam Conference in July of 1945, was to return as many people as possible to their country of origin. This meant, for instance, that millions of Germans were returned from Eastern Europe to Germany. Some of those had been forced under Hitler's regime to live outside Germany. But some, who had migrated to places like Poland and Czechoslovakia and had established homes and created cultures of substance, even prior to National Socialism, had to give up their farms or urban homes to return to Germany. According to one estimate, as many as 14,400 Germans per day were being forced to abandon their homes after the war.

Similar policies extended to the Jewish population whom the Germans already had displaced or imprisoned in concentration camps in Eastern Europe. The Allies also agreed that Soviet citizens who had migrated during the war, either for safety or to escape political tyranny, also would need to return to the Soviet Union. Over two million Russians resettled in territories under Communist rule. These policies also forced over two million Poles to return to Poland, taking the place of the former German occupants. Meanwhile, half a million Ukrainians, Belarusians and others were deported from Poland to the Soviet Union. Going in the other direction were hundreds of thousands of Ukrainians, Estonians, Latvians, Lithuanians, Croats, and others, fearful of reprisals for wartime activities, who fled westwards from all over eastern Europe, hoping to find a home in the United States or Canada. The British government forced some unlucky Serbs and Croats to return to Yugoslavia. Around 2,000 of these refugees were executed summarily under Tito's regime.

Even during the war, the international community took steps to try to address the displacement of peoples caused by the global conflict. In 1943, the United States led the way (with forty-four nations signing on) by creating the United Nations Relief and Rehabilitation Administration (UNRRA). Its purpose was to assist displaced persons in returning to their home countries. Prisoners from concentration camps and forced labor camps occupied most of UNRRA's attention. In 1946, the agency retooled as the International Refugee Organization. By 1950, two years after the formation of the United Nations, assistance to the Europeans uprooted by World War II came from the United Nations High Commission for Refugees. These bodies were permitted to act strictly for humanitarian reasons. In addition to the emerging Cold War between the United States and Western Europe on the one side and the Soviet Union and its Communist satellites, finding a home for refugees also depended on whether a host nation needed labor for its work force. For instance, Britain and Australia granted many Poles the right of permanent settlement to work in the mining industries. Meanwhile, the creation of the state of Israel in 1948 became an important step in accommodating Jewish Europeans.

Through the work of these international agencies, a definition of refugee emerged. Under international law, a refugee is someone who is outside his or her home and has a well-founded fear of persecution based on race, religion, nationality, political opinion, or membership in a particular social group. In 1951, the United Nations codified this definition and it remained in force until 1967 revisions expanded it to include refugees beyond the scope of those peoples whose lives had been disrupted by World War II.

According to this definition, my family and I were refugees. We were no longer in our home, which was Split. We had left Croatia because we not only feared but had experienced persecution — my father had been imprisoned by the Italians. And because my father was Serbian, he was suspect at least to the Croatian Fascists, which should have qualified as persecution based on religion and ethnicity. Also, because of the Novakovics' Royalist sympathies and my uncle's service in the Yugoslav Royal Army, our fears also extended to differences based on political opinions. Even so, the legal definition of refugee did not exist until almost a decade after we left Split for Trieste.

Once we acquired papers from the Italian governing authorities in Trieste, we were technically, under the provisions of the later law, no longer refugees. By the end of the war, it was a very good thing that we acquired legal status through the Vatican which gave us access to visas for migrating to South America. Without those papers, the policies of the international bodies likely would have forced us back to Yugoslavia according to the logic of repatriation. And without those papers we would have experienced a fate similar to Serbs and Croats under Tito or to anti-communist refugees from Czechoslovakia and Poland, where the rule of Communism made repatriation deadly.

Without the help of the international agencies that emerged to address the problem of dislocated European peoples, we had managed to make our way from Croatia to Italy. And then again on our own, with the generous assistance of American military personnel and the Vatican, we arranged to find a passage to South America while we hoped to move up the list of people waiting to gain visas for the United States. Our experience proved that it was possible for displaced people, even if not qualifying legally as refugees, to move from war-torn and politically divided European nations to a new home across the Atlantic. Ironically, we benefitted from not relying on the helping hand of refugee agencies for in some cases, it resulted in summary executions. The rules governing Germans, Russians, Poles, and Yugoslavs could well have forced us to return to a homeland that could no longer provide the peace, safety, and security in what we had called home.

Part Two
Becoming an American

❧

CHAPTER 28

Bon Voyage

K nowing what I now know, I am amazed to think that my family and I had so little trouble finding passage on an ocean liner for our journey to South America. Prior to World War I, at least three ship lines offered service between Genoa and Argentina: the La Italia, the Compania Lloyd Italiano, and the Hamburg Amerika Line, most of which sailed twice a month on trips that lasted approximately three weeks. But during World War I and World War II, ships became a precious asset for the rival national powers, and the home nation often commandeered a shipping company's vessels to transport soldiers and retrofitted them for the demands of war. For instance, when the British, at the beginning of World War II, faced a shortage of warships, they expropriated a number of passenger lines for use as armed merchant cruisers. These ships were equipped with naval guns and then deployed for reconnaissance or envoy escort. Although slower than most naval ships, these converted ships could also endure harsher weather and so were invaluable for protecting other vessels or seaways.

The need for ships during war meant that some of the premier European ocean liner companies went out of business or took years to recover. The Hamburg Amerika Line, for example, lost all of its fifty-six ships during World War II, either sunk during the conflict or confiscated by European powers. The Potsdam Treaty established terms for the company to resume its commercial activities but the line was not up and running until 1951. That was six years too late for our needs.

Another consideration that did not occur to me then — but must have to my parents — was the danger of sea travel. The bottom of the Atlantic Ocean may not be covered with sunken vessels but no doubt parts of it are cluttered with ships that succumbed to bad weather, errors in navigation, fires on board, or warfare. On January 30, 1945, a Soviet submarine torpedoed the *Wilhelm Gustloff*, a German ship, in the Baltic Sea. It was the worst maritime disaster in terms of the loss of life since the sinking of the *Titanic*. In the disaster, over 5,300 German refugees, wounded soldiers, and crew who were escaping the German war zone lost their lives. We did not have to worry about threats from artillery thanks to the end of war. But the elements, human miscalculation, or defects in the ship were still possible to cause the sinking of any ship. About a decade after we left Europe, in the summer of 1956, off the island of Nantucket, the famous sinking of the *Andrea Doria* took place when the *SS Stockholm* collided with it. Forty-six people died on board the *Andrea Doria* and five were killed on the *Stockholm*, a remarkably low figure considering that lifeboats on board the *Doria* were inaccessible.

None of these considerations, however, entered my mind as I excitedly boarded the ship for the three-week voyage from Genoa to Buenos Aires. Twenty-one days was a long time to be cooped up on a 22,000-ton liner with 200 other passengers. It was designed to house about 60. And most of the amenities were designed more for adults than for boys. But Paul and I were able to take advantage of the games on the sports deck. Shuffleboard was our favorite.

During one of our contests, we saw the difficulties that could afflict passengers and crews even when the weather was good and the ship was sailing smoothly. Out of the corner of my eye, I noticed a big block of color fall from one of the upper decks, almost like a big bag. My brother and I ran to the rail to see what it was. I discovered that one of the male passengers had jumped overboard, apparently hoping to take his life. I started to throw life preservers to him. When he hit the water, he must have reconsidered and eventually grasped one of the preservers before one of the crew members was able to extend a line to him and pull him back on board. Although I felt good about helping to save this man's life, I could not enjoy the moment for very long. One of the ship's officers informed me, quite loudly and excitedly, of my error in throwing several of those life preservers for the sake of one person. In fact, the ship had to circle back on its route to retrieve as many of those preservers as the crew could. I thought to myself that I would do it again if I had to.

This incident, however, provided only minor discomfort compared to what I experienced at our first port of call in Las Palmas on the Canary Islands. When we disembarked, I saw plants and fruits that I had never seen before. Bananas particularly were appealing. I tried my first and loved it. So I proceeded to eat more. By the time I was full, I had eaten almost two dozen bananas. Back on board the ship, I got severe abdominal pain, throat ache, and cramps, from ingesting an excessive amount of potassium. According to the United States Food and Drug Administrations Recommended Daily Allowances, 4,000 milligrams of potassium may cause poisoning. The USFDA also estimates that an average banana has 400 milligrams of potassium. It does not take a math major to figure out that I was in serious pain and in real danger of potassium poisoning. Of course, not helping matters was my recent bout of appendicitis and peritonitis.

As sick as I was, the weather turned rough and I also came down with a bout of sea sickness. This was a blessing in disguise since it forced me to reject some of the bananas that I had eaten. Also helping was the ocean liner's nurse who treated me by giving me pills that reduced my heart rate and breathing. There were no doctors on board.

It was not the most pleasant voyage of my life. In fact, it bore too many similarities to some of my experiences in Italy during the war. But we were safe, free, and excited about the prospects of a new life. If the war had not discouraged me, a couple of difficult episodes on the voyage to Buenos Aires were not going to prevent me from looking forward to our new life in America (whether South or North). Somehow, I was convinced we would eventually get to the U.S.A.

CHAPTER 29

Life Under Peron

After a stop in Sao Paulo, we finally arrived in Buenos Aires, a city that was very European, and not simply because of all the Europeans who had either migrated to or sought asylum in Argentina. There was a complicated history during the nineteenth century which saw this country carve out political independence from Spanish control, and national consolidation which involved rivalry with Brazil and the loss of Paraguay (1842). By 1900, Argentina, a federation of twenty-three provinces, had emerged as one of the ten richest nations in the world and the second largest nation in South America (next to Brazil). The main source of Argentina's wealth was its agricultural interior, though France and Britain invested significantly in select industries. The English were interested especially in building and maintaining a rail system that greatly assisted the nation's development and gave the British government significant influence in Argentinian affairs. At the same time, the nation attracted immigrants from Europe, primarily Spain, Italy, and some from Germany.

Buenos Aires was the beneficiary of much of Europe's fiscal and human capital. The city became a hub for the nation's rail system and the port through which Argentina exported its produce and raw materials. The nation had declared itself neutral during World War II, but by the end of the conflict had become an important source of food for the

Allies. The European presence within Buenos Aires gave it a cosmopolitan flavor and it developed in ways that rivaled Europe's capitals. The Colón Theater became one of the world's top venues for opera, and the city was home to sophisticated radio, movie, and theater productions. City planners laid out its main avenues during the early twentieth century according to European standards. Buenos Aires was also responsible for the first subway system in South America, and the construction of South America's tallest skyscraper.

When we arrived, we did not feel like we had entered a foreign world. Buenos Aires may have not felt like home, but it was close enough to what we knew in pre-war Europe to feel very comfortable. In fact, my father, with special pleading from my older sister, Deana, decided to petition the Argentinian authorities for permission for us to stay there instead of proceeding to Paraguay. All along, our ultimate goal was to relocate all the way to the United States. Thanks to Colonel Jager's efforts back in Milano, we were on a waiting list that was supposed to take five years. The question was where to wait until our number was called. Buenos Aires looked like the best option. It did not hurt that the history of Italian immigrants to Argentina made it relatively easy for us to use the language that we had learned to speak flawlessly during the war.

By the time of our arrival in the fall of 1945, Buenos Aires was experiencing many of the social tensions that afflicted other urban industrial centers. The city started to attract migrants from the nation's provinces as well as the neighboring countries. Shanty towns cropped up around the city's industrial areas as early as the 1940s. This development put strains on the city. Division between the native poor and wealthy elites also developed.

The conditions that workers faced contributed the following that Juan Peron created to gain election as president in the year after our arrival. He was already vice president in 1945, thanks to his role in the military coup of 1943. He also wore the hats of Secretary of War during the international conflict and, in addition, was the Minister of

Labor. Adding to his appeal was Eva Duarte, Peron's mistress until their wedding in October of 1945. We were in Buenos Aires at the time and saw some of the festivities but our attention was much more focused on trying to establish a home and find work than it was on the affairs of Argentina's new government. A Socialist, Peron took a decidedly pro-labor position in his policies. The militarily-dominated government saw him as a threat and forced him to resign. Four days later, on October 15, 1945, the authorities imprisoned him. But mass protests, organized in part by "Evita," forced Peron's release from jail after two days. By the time of the next presidential elections in February, 1946, Peron's Socialist Party beat his closest competitor by eleven percent, receiving over fifty-three percent of the votes. The election could not really be certified — stories abounded regarding illegal voting which was rampant.

The peso lost seventy percent of its value during our stay. The city seemed chaotic, even to a teenager. People roamed the streets in groups and many seemed to be unemployed. They would actually go about the city in pajamas which was a sign of protest against the elites and middle-class who wore suits and business attire. The word for them was "shirtless." It was a signal that they belonged to the working class. The problem was that none of these people wanted to work. I still cannot believe how inefficient the city seemed. Although Peron came from a military career, he seemed to know nothing about the advantages of routine and efficiency. At the same time, his government came up with rules for everything. It seemed as if you could not take a drink of water without having to comply with a regulation. The inevitable result was that almost everyone disregarded the rules. (On later trips to Buenos Aires I knew a lot more about the workings of societies and economies and continued to be amazed that the city functioned.)

Peron's administration and the problems his ineffectual policies caused were good reasons for not wanting to settle in Buenos Aires for the long term. But in the short-run it was a welcome respite from the real chaos we had known first-hand in Europe.

CHAPTER 30

Making a Home in Buenos Aires

The Serbian Diaspora is the phrase used to account for the large number of Serbs who now live outside the former Yugoslavia. *According to recent estimates, as many as 3.5 million Serbs live in parts of the world other than Serbia, Croatia, Montenegro, Bosnia, and Herzegovina. During World War I, many Serbs migrated to the east, to Czechoslovakia, Russia and Ukraine. Others at various points in the twentieth century, moved to the United States, Canada, Australia, and New Zealand for economic reasons. Some were forced to leave for Western Europe because of the policies of the Ottoman Turks. One last factor in this dispersion of Serbs, much more recent, was the Balkan wars of the 1990s. Meanwhile, centuries-old Serbian communities exist and prosper in such countries as Austria, Czech Republic, Greece, Hungary, Italy, Romania, Russia, Poland, Slovakia, Turkey, the Ukraine, and the United States. In all of these cases, the Serbian Diaspora was the result of either voluntary departure, coercion, and/or forced migrations or expulsions. This means that the countries with the highest concentrations of Serbian and Croatian populations are countries like the United States, Canada, Brazil, Australia, and most countries in western Europe. Some of the cities with the greatest numbers of Serbs are Budapest, Istanbul, London, Paris, Trieste, Vienna, Chicago, Phoenix, Los Angeles, and Toronto. Argentina and Buenos Aires are not included on

unable to verify

the lists of large Serbian populations. Even Denmark and Sweden have more Serbs than Argentina.

Our experience in Buenos Aires offered a different perspective on the Serbian Diaspora. We were not surrounded by Serbs but we did establish ties that would be pivotal for our family both in the short and long-term. In fact, my younger sister, Gordana, mother, and father are all buried in Argentina. The reason has everything to do with the relationships we formed during our three years in Buenos Aires while we waited for visas to the United States.

The most important of those ties was Gordana's romance and marriage to Dragui Vukojcic, also known as Mr. Dragui, a Serb who came from a highly successful and prosperous family in the old country. The Vukojcic family had become wealthy in textile and carpet manufacturing. They also owned a plant that constructed airplanes, the only such facility in the Balkans during the 1930s. During the war, family members escaped to Turkey and then returned to Yugoslavia to fight the Communists and Tito. Thanks to Winston Churchill's miscalculation and Britain's decision to back Tito instead of the Chetnik leader, Draža Mihailovic (a difficult decision, mind you, since Mihailovic was not innocent of the ethnic hatreds that plagued Yugoslavia), Dragui and his brothers had to flee the country and they, like us, found their way to South America. Dragui's brother had been a senior officer in the Chetnik forces in charge of defending Belgrade and leading the resistance to Tito. And like my father, he was on the list of Tito's enemies of state to be "executed on sight." So relentless were the Communists that they tried to hunt Dragui's brother down in Brazil, where he had settled. When he heard of the order from a friend, he went to the Yugoslavian embassy in Rio de Janeiro and told the officials that if anything happened to him, the officials and their families would be killed. That put an end to the Communist threat, at least for him and his family.

Within a year of our arrival in Buenos Aires, Gordana and Dragui were married and they remained in Argentina for the rest of their lives.

Over time, with important assistance from my sister, Dragui became a very successful and wealthy businessman. He invented machines to make carpeting and various textiles. His business eventually dominated the Latin American carpet market and grew into an international enterprise. They had three daughters and two sons — a wonderful family, and were very generous to my parents, flying them first class to Argentina for regular visits once the rest of our family settled in the United States. Dragui was also a devout member of the Serbian Orthodox Church and gave generously to the construction of Serbian churches in Buenos Aires.

I worked for Dragui for a short while in Buenos Aires. He was a brilliant engineer. He was a good man and as we worked together we developed a strong relationship. I continued to work in his company part-time while trying to finish my high school education.

I did not think of the business as a Serbian enterprise. My family and I mixed easily with the rest of the Europeans in Buenos Aires and because we spoke fluent Italian, some of our neighbors may have thought that we were Italian natives. But we were Serbian and we established Serbian ties in Buenos Aires.

CHAPTER 31

Going to American High School

With the end of war came a return to normal life. We were settled in Buenos Aires and were able to resume some of the activities that had characterized our life in Split. For Paul and me, this meant going back to school, something we had not done for the better part of four years. We were still living off the surplus gold we had taken out of Croatia but it was running out. So in addition to school, Paul and I found jobs; mine, of course, was working for my brother-in-law in the company's plant. But we were also teenagers and needed to start to prepare for the rest of our lives, which required considerations regarding a course of study that would prepare us for college and equip us for careers.

The academic institution my parents chose was the American International School. Founded in 1936 it was and remains (now called Lincoln American High School) the school where American diplomats and business people who were residing in the Argentinian capital, sent their children. To this day, the "Asociación Escuelas Lincoln" is the recommended school by the U.S. Department of State's Office of Overseas Schools. The curriculum at the school was designed to prepare students for admission to American and European universities. Although recognized by the Argentinian department of education, today the school is accredited by the U.S. agency, the Southern Association of Colleges and Schools.

Of course, I was well behind my age group when I started to take classes. To make up for the lost time during the war, the school's administrators gave Paul and me a grueling series of tests that enabled us to join the class appropriate to our age level. They also supplied us with textbooks that we took home to study on our own in preparation for the tests. One of the funniest incidents — at least to me — during our studies was our preparation for the exam in biology. Paul was the better student, always studying hard for tests. I had never opened this textbook. Instead, I relied on Paul, who tutored me in the material. Unlike my experience in Split's schools, I loved the high school in Buenos Aires and enjoyed learning biology. But I was also willing to let Paul show me the ropes, since I was working part-time for my brother-in-law. When it came time for us to take the exam, I received an A and Paul only managed a B. It may be the only time that I outperformed him in school. I guess what helped me the most was the need to memorize a number of formulas, and memorization always came easily to me. Anyway, when Paul eventually entered a difficult program in engineering, I enjoyed reminding him that I had received a better grade than he did in biology.

I also loved learning English at the American High School. We had already started to learn the language back in Italy, though we did so surreptitiously since English-speakers were under watch of the Italian authorities. My sister, Deana, knew the language well and had started teaching us English as early as our stay in Viggiu, which was an obvious part of our usefulness to the British and American military police in Milano after the war. But our English in Italy was far from grammatically correct and one of the reasons for choosing the American High School was to improve our facility with the language and make the transition to the United States easier. I was never able to get rid of my accent, though when I spoke Italian I could do so in ways that rivaled the natives. Obviously, our lives during the war depended on being able to fit in and on speaking Italian well, a need that was not as pressing when we learned English. Notwithstanding the accent, I excelled in geography and math.

In addition to classes, the American High School had a full extra-curricular program that included athletics. Here my speed offered me another way to excel. I joined the track team and became something of a star. My best event was the 100-yard dash. I did not have to train that much to beat all of my competitors; I was blessed with natural speed and polished that gift running during the war.

Between classes and athletics I fit in well at the school. This turned out to be important not just for Paul and me but also for the family. One of our classmates was the son of the United States Naval attaché to Buenos Aires, Captain Harold Thomas Deutermann. The American High School was designed precisely for families like the Deutermanns and making connections with American officials was another reason my parents selected the American school for us. As it turned out, our friendship with the Deutermanns would be crucial to our move to the United States.

In the meantime, my life had returned to the kind that most adolescent boys in western industrialized countries were experiencing. Granted, I did not know where we would ultimately settle. But our basic needs of food, shelter, and clothing no longer a worry, on top of which we had the luxury of going to school, having friends, and playing sports. During our stay in Ancona, Feltre and Varese, I could never have imagined this kind of life.

CHAPTER 32

Another American in a High Place

As valuable as the education at the American High School was for Paul and me, even more significant were the friendships we made. The Deutermanns were an example of this. A native of White Plains, New York, Captain Deutermann graduated from the Naval Academy in 1927. After various assignments during the 1930s, he served as chief engineer on the anti-aircraft cruiser, San Juan, in the South Pacific in response to the Japanese attack on Pearl Harbor. In 1943 he assumed command of a newly built destroyer, the Cogswell, and remained in the Pacific theater for the rest of the war. After the war, the Navy assigned him to Argentina, where he served for two years and had broad powers in military, political, and intelligence matters. He worked in the Navy until 1965, achieving the rank of Vice Admiral, commanding the Second Fleet in Norfolk, Virginia and the Eastern Sea Frontier. After retiring from the Navy, he taught mathematics at the University of Florida in Gainesville.

He had three sons, all of whom entered the military. His son, David, was in class with my brother Paul. After becoming friends with Paul and me, Captain Deutermann expressed a desire to meet my family, and subsequently volunteered to help us navigate a route to the United States.

Meeting Captain Deutermann made a huge impression on Paul and me. For a while, both of us wanted to serve in the U.S. Navy. Paul did.

I found another path into the U.S. military. Paul also kept up with Deutermann's son, David. He eventually went to the Naval Academy and became an Admiral. While my brother was stationed in Connecticut, he received an invitation from David to visit at the fleet command in Naples. Paul received and accepted the royal treatment that only Admirals have at their disposal.

Another one of Deutermann's sons, whom we did not know very well because he was several years behind us and not in the high school, had an even more notable career than either his brothers or his father. However, his fame came not from the Navy. P. T. Deutermann followed in his father's footsteps and had a distinguished career as a captain in the Navy. During twenty-six years of service, he earned nineteen medals and decorations, and commanded the *USS Tattnall* between 1981 and 1983, directed the arms control office for the Joint Chiefs of Staff, and served as a technical delegate to the United Nations.

But his fame came in retirement when he moved to Georgia and launched a writing career. His first spy thriller, *Scorpion in the Sea* (1992) pitted a maverick Navy captain against a Libyan sub that is dispatched off the coast of Florida in retaliation for the 1986 bombing of Tripoli. Soon he got an agent and went on to write thirteen additional spy novels, three of which received interest from Hollywood.

Clearly, the Deutermanns were a family to reckon with. His generous assistance was decisive in our attempt to secure papers to settle in the United States. But in the larger scheme of our lives, Captain Deutermann was just one of many American soldiers in Europe and in South America who were extremely kind, decent, and honorable to us. Making the acquaintance with people like them who spoke volumes about the United States, made us all the more eager to find a home there.

CHAPTER 33

Should We Go to the United States?

In the fall of 1949, our number for a visa to the United States came up earlier than expected. Instead of waiting the entire five years, we gained permission to enter the United States after roughly four and one-half years from the time we had first applied in Milano. Undoubtedly, various people's good words for us had helped. Whether or not you believe in God, it did seem that some higher power was looking out for my family and me.

The news came at a good time. We were on the verge of running out of money. The gold that we had brought out of Yugoslavia to Trieste had sustained us almost eight years, a long time to be without any real income. It had paid for permits and visas, for bus, train, and boat trips, for hotel rooms, apartment and villa rentals, for food when it was available, for high school tuition, and even for a trans-Atlantic voyage. Most important, it saved my father's life. If my father had been able to keep his second suitcase of gold, we might have had enough money for several more years in Buenos Aires. But that was not the case. The family needed jobs to make a living but fast.

At this point Paul and I made a decision that would be decisive for the entire family. Paul had applied for a job as a cabin boy scrubbing the cabins and the deck for the Moore-McCormack Ship Lines, a firm that operated a variety of merchant ships and ocean liners. Like the European companies, Moore-McCormack's business was seriously affected by World War II and many of their vessels had been commandeered by the United States. But they returned to do a brisk business after the war, operating all the way until 1982. Moore-McCormack was the most obvious way for us to travel to New York City. My plan was to work on a cargo ship headed for the U.S. and then stay there. Paul and I were finally going to the United States. Hallelujah! I was thrilled beyond description.

When we told our parents of our decision they were reluctant. They did not want us to go to the United States alone — keep in mind, I was barely 16 years old — and they thought we should remain together as a family. Paul and I had no intention of breaking up the family, but we were intent on living in the United States. At the time it was possible, at least we thought so, for adolescents like us to be admitted and find jobs and a place to live.

Still, our determination placed our parents in a real dilemma. All along we had wanted to go to America and make a home there. For that reason, Paul and I did not think we were doing anything out of the ordinary. Our papers had been approved and we had simply found a way to travel to the United States — a way that would not only save money but earn some. But our sister Gordana, now married to a businessman whose company was thriving, obviously would not be able to go with us if we moved to the United States. To keep the family together would mean honoring Gordana's marriage and remaining in Buenos Aires

For seven years we had endured war and migration while finding ways to stay together as a family. The war experience only deepened our bonds. The war could not break us up, even if it did briefly at times when we went in separate directions with each parent during artillery attacks or in a combat environment. As much as our purpose during the war was to stay together as a family, the point of migrating to America was to find a safe and free home. Gordana achieved that in Argentina. The rest of the family was about to see what the United States had in store. Our long-range objective was finally being achieved. Thank God!

CHAPTER 34

Coming to America

We said goodbye to Gordana and Dragui in early December of 1949. It was a painful departure. Gordana was very close to my father in particular. When the family divided during bombing raids, Gordana and Paul went with my father, while Deana and I went with my mother. The purpose of these separations was to be sure that at least part of the family might survive. But as distressing as leaving Gordana was, nothing would keep us from wanting to be in the U.S.A.

America had the most opportunities in the world at this time, and we felt a great debt to the efforts of the U.S. soldiers during the war, not to mention the assistance from Colonel Jager and Admiral Deutermann. So, we boarded one of Moore-McCormack's smallest and cheapest cargo ships and set off for New York City. The trip lasted twenty-one days, about as long as the one from Genoa to Buenos Aires, though this time I avoided a meal of bananas. In fact, I did not get sick at all.

When we entered Hudson Bay, we began to see the Statue of Liberty. At first it was a white speck and then as it got bigger and bigger from our view on the ship's deck, the excitement of coming to the United States for the first time sank in, not just for my family and me, but for the rest of the passengers. What impressed me when I first saw New York City's skyline was not the size or scale of the structures since Buenos Aires is a sophisticated city and could rival other modern cities in appearance.

What was impressive was what New York City represented. It stood for freedom, security, and opportunity — all the things that had only been a dream while we sought safety and hoped for peace during our sojourn in Italy. I was so elated by the city of New York that tears welled up for the rest of the voyage. God bless the U.S.A.

We arrived at Ellis Island on Christmas Eve, 1949. It was still the United States' busiest inspection station for immigrants. The buildings for processing immigrants were constructed in 1892, two years after the federal government first assumed control for regulating the "teaming masses yearning to breathe free." For its first thirty years, the facility was largely a check point for newcomers to America. After 1924, when the United States significantly restricted immigration, Ellis Island took on the functions of a detention and deportation center; its officials and staff were then more concerned to prevent easy access to the United States. But after World War II and the heavy influx of refugees into America, Ellis Island returned to its old form as a place large enough and easily accessible for ships to handle the tens of thousands of immigrants coming to America. That Christmas Eve when we went through the lines and check point, our experience was much more like going through customs than a border checkpoint. We filled out the forms and answered the officials' questions without a hitch. We were the last group to go through the lines that day. We were soon on board a ferry, bound for the Bowery.

Officials at Ellis Island advised us to go to Times Square in Manhattan. So after taking the ferry, we next looked for a bus to go from the Bowery to the center of the city. The scene of a family of five, loaded down with dilapidated suitcases, taking a public bus must have looked humorous to passersby. But anyone accustomed to seeing immigrants fresh off a boat from Ellis Island would have also thought our appearance common. By now we had all of our belongings, stuffed into four old leather suitcases, and needed to find cheap accommodations. We were tired, and struggled with the cumbersome bags. But because it was Christmas Eve, the buses had fewer passengers than normal and could accommodate the newcomers.

When we disembarked from the bus, a very different experience, mind you, from our bus trip from Ancona through Bolognia to Maggio, we needed to find a hotel. The best room available was an average flop house that had its fair share of ne'er do wells and unsavory boarders.

Mike's Father, Branko Novakovic, Dec. 17, 1957, returning from Buenos Aires to New York.
This photo best describes Branko's sentiments

We took one room and all of us went to sleep, my brother and I on the floor. The flop house and Times Square were not the most congenial of spots to spend our first night in the United States. But as I went to sleep that night I had one image on my mind that lifted my spirits. As we had walked from the ferry to the bus stop I saw a very elegant, pretty young woman, carrying several big shopping bags, with a bounce in her step, clearly anticipating the merriment of the evening and Christmas Day. That was a great sight. It promised a brighter future for this family of immigrants. Maybe we too would soon go beyond celebrating our safe passage to even enjoying the ways that Americans celebrated their holidays. ***God Bless America.***

CHAPTER 35

Making a Living and a Life in America

Our appearance as typical immigrants, disembarking from the ferry and cramming on to a city bus, was just the first act in our drama as newcomers to New York City. We stayed at the hotel in Times Square for only a few nights. After making some contacts, my parents moved us to Orange, New Jersey. A family we had met in Buenos Aires, through the American High School, gave my parents the name of friends in the New York City suburb who provided a place to stay while we tried to find work.

By that time our money basically was gone and all of us needed to work since no one in the family could command a job to support all of us. Family solidarity as a team of workers was the second act of our drama.

We did not stay in Orange for long because we soon discovered that the suburbs had far fewer jobs than the city, and the commute from Orange to New York City was costly. Orange is about fifteen miles west of Manhattan and the city was accessible only by a commuter train or an automobile, which we were in no position to purchase. My father actually made contact with the vice president of Irving Trust Company, a big bank located at 1 Wall Street in a beautiful Art Deco skyscraper built in 1931. The friend tried to help us find jobs in New Jersey. I applied to a gas station but I was not old enough. My father did pump gas for a brief time. But we soon learned that there were better prospects in the city.

So we moved to an apartment in the Bronx on East 201st Street. From here, all of us found jobs to help pay for the apartment and other expenses. My father worked initially as a bellhop for a hotel in Manhattan. His English was not as good as his children's and this held him back initially. But he became more fluent the longer he worked there and when the manager discovered my father's background in banking, he moved him into the hotel's accounting office. Like other immigrant families, my mother also needed to work. She took a job as a seamstress in the city's garment district where she sewed slacks.

My brother continued to work for Moore-McCormack in their New York offices so that he could finish his high school education. Deana found a job in the New York offices of Shell Oil Company. Meanwhile, I heard about an opening at the Irving Trust Company, the bank of my father's friend. I learned that they needed page boys. I decided to apply without trying to have anyone pull strings. To my surprise, they did not inquire about my age. Even more surprising was their decision to hire me.

I loved the job, partly because the building was extraordinarily beautiful. The lobby had the stunningly ornate detail of the best Art Deco interiors. You entered the Reception Hall directly from Wall Street, one of the most spectacular commercial spaces in New York, with opulent colors that contrasted with the building's exterior. The lobby-reception area, three stories in height, featured glass mosaics, manufactured in Berlin, that moved from a dark red at the base to orange at the ceiling. Offsetting this design in glass was a web-like pattern of gold. Each floor had dark wood paneling and thick carpets. I felt surrounded by wealth, not simply from the customers who deposited and invested their funds with the company, but also by the building itself.

My job, which took me to almost all of the building's floors, was to deliver communications and mail between the company's top executives. As I recall, they had some forty vice presidents who needed to communicate with each other across the various departments, dispersed on different floors of 1 Wall Street. Since this was an era before computers or faxes, their letters and memos needed to delivered by hand. I had an hour to make my deliveries. Because of my speed (again), I usually completed the assigned round in twenty minutes to a half-hour. This gave me free time, usually to do my high school homework, but also to admire the building's interiors and sometimes the female staff. My abilities as a speedy deliverer also gave me more time for lunch. This was a meal I loved, not simply because the food was great and free, an extremely generous perk, but also because the cafeteria was as beautiful as the rest of the building.

My salary started at twenty cents per hour. Within a few months, I earned a raise and was making twenty-eight cents per hour. Today, that would be the equivalent of roughly $2.50. That is not a lot of money, even for an immigrant. But when we added up all the streams of revenue from the five of us working in New York and living in the Bronx, we were able to pay the rent, afford food and clothes, and take the first step up the ladder of success in the United States. Paul and I advanced the most in our movement from riches to rags and back to riches. We were the youngest and had the most time for the opportunities that the United States offered immigrants. But even though my parents experienced a real loss of status, and my sister, Deana, faced many more limitations as a young single woman, none of us regretted our decision to live in the United States.

I felt a strong obligation to America and decided I would do my best to repay the country, and I did.

America —
Land of the Free. Home of the Brave.

CHAPTER 36

"I Am from New York"

When I eventually went to college, people sometimes asked me where I was from. It was a natural question, even if a little annoying. My accent gave away that I was not "from" America. What became frustrating was that after I answered this question with, "I'm from New York," was the question that inevitably followed — "Where were you born?" The answer to that question was obviously Yugoslavia but it was also a complicated response because most Americans in the 1950s only knew about Yugoslavia in the context of Tito, Communism, and the Cold War. Aside from possibly having to explain Yugoslavian history, I preferred the answer "I'm from New York," because I was. During my brief time in the United States, I experienced and identified with New York City in ways that few Americans, even New Yorkers, had.

My ordinary day, once we moved to the Bronx, involved rising at 6:30 AM so I could make the commute to Wall Street in time for the beginning of the office day at 9:00 AM. I took the Third Ave. elevated train, a line that no longer exists (it ceased operation in 1955), from the Bronx to mid-town where I transferred at 40th Street in Manhattan to another elevated train that took me to Chatham Square — City Hall — where I walked or ran the rest of the eight blocks into the Bowery and Wall Street. It was a long commute — almost an hour on the train alone. But that was valuable time I used to do homework.

After working a full day at the Irving Trust Company, I retraced my route back to the Bronx where I went to night school at Fordham High School, located near Fordham University. At the time, New Yorkers could receive a full high school education at night. From six o'clock until roughly ten-thirty each weeknight I took classes at the high school. During my first two years in the United States I finished my junior and senior years of high school, in effect, completing the course of study I had started in Buenos Aires. By the time I arrived back at our apartment on 201st Street it was eleven o'clock and I was worn out. Every weekday during the school year I repeated this routine.

I decided to push myself in this fashion because I wanted to go to college. The only way to get there was to finish high school. And the primary reason for going to college was the one that sends most Americans to higher education — the best path to a successful career was through the preparation and training received at college.

I can't say that I was the best student. My brother Paul was exceptional and he eventually studied engineering at the Rensselaer Polytechnic Institute. But I was diligent and kept up with my school assignments, especially using the commute to and from the Bronx. I also had time during the workday at Irving Trust.

With a pace like this, eight hours of work each day and four hours of class each night, I had little time for socializing. I suppose many of my classmates came from immigrant backgrounds but I did not know that. I had no time to meet them. I did listen to the radio some and became familiar with the big band music of the time. I was especially fond of Bing Crosby's voice and recordings. Even though the Bronx Bombers (Yankees) were playing in my neighborhood, the only sport I found appealing was college football, and that was an interest that remained dormant until I eventually enrolled at college.

My only real form of recreation during those very busy years was eating. With my schedule I had few meals at home. So aside from those abundant and free meals in the cafeteria at the Irving Trust Company,

I ate many suppers at the Horn & Hardart restaurants that dotted New York City's map. These were essentially the first fast food restaurants in the United States. The German-born Joseph Horn and the New Orleans-native, Frank Hardart opened their first establishment in Philadelphia in 1888. In 1902, they introduced to the United States, inspired by a similar endeavor in Berlin, the idea of an Automat, a coin operated vending machine that offered freshly prepared dishes and sandwiches. By the time of Horn's death in 1941, the chain had 157 retail shops and restaurants in the Philadelphia and New York areas and served 500,000 patrons a day. During the 1940s and the 1950s, more than fifty New York Horn & Hardart restaurants served 350,000 customers a day. I was one of them and enjoyed practically every meal I ate there, even if it meant that I studied while I finished my dinner.

Within my family, I was not the only one working hard. In fact, when I graduated from high school in the spring of 1951, no one from my family came to the ceremony. This didn't bother me. I had no reason to be sentimental about the occasion. It was simply part of my preparation to enter American society and make the United States my lasting home. Middle-class families in the United States might have looked upon a son or daughter's graduation from high school as a rite of passage. For us, it was almost as ordinary as the comings and goings of the Third Avenue Elevated.

During my senior year, I started to look into colleges and universities. I had decided that I wanted to enter the U.S. military, thanks to the powerful impressions made on me by the American military police in Milano. The helping hands supplied by Colonel Jager in Italy and Admiral Deutermann in Argentina were also a factor in my decision. The rapport that I developed with the G.I.s in Italy after the war was an experience that I also hoped to continue. My desire to serve in the military meant that I looked for a college or university with an R.O.T.C. program. The institutions that were relatively close to New York City that I heard most about were Princeton University, Cornell University, and Syracuse University. Because Cornell did not have an R.O.T.C. program, I did not apply there. Princeton did, but my grades were not good enough to gain admittance to an Ivy League institution — though I had little awareness of what an Ivy League university was or what such American academic institutions represented. That left Syracuse as the only option.

The university on Lake Onondaga and founded by Methodists accepted my application. It, too, was a good university and my grades were probably about average for the applicants. My focus was less on the course of study than on training to become a military officer. But this was a time, the fall of 1951, when lots of returning Korean veterans were going to school on the G.I. Bill. Maybe my own experience during the war helped distinguish my application from others. Even more important, as it turned out, was another part of my past. Syracuse was the home to a Croatian faculty member, Ivan Meštrovic, a world-famous sculptor and a family friend from our hometown of Split. His presence at the university and willingness to support my application were important parts of my decision to go to Syracuse.

Ivan Meštrovic

So, even though questions about my home and place of birth were annoying at times, I could not escape my past either in Croatia or New York City. As it turned out, both were important for the next stage of my life.

CHAPTER 37

Broken But Not Severed

Immigrants who seek refuge in a new country, as we did when we came to New York City in 1949, hope to make a new life for themselves. All people bring with them belongings (however modest), affections and loyalties, and names and languages derived from the country of origin. Even so, unless an immigrant has family ties in the new country, he must start all over again. This was certainly my family's experience. We had no one providing us with the basic necessities or guidance. No government welfare agency, city, state, or federal, was there to welcome us and assist in finding a place to stay that first night, or point us to a kitchen with a hot meal. We had to find our way almost entirely on our own, and we did. We were not expecting nor wanted a handout from anyone. So relieved were we to find legal passage to a land of liberty and opportunity that we were thrilled simply by our prospects in the United States.

I soon learned, however, especially when I embarked on a life at college, independent from my parents, that there were contacts and associations I had forged in the old world that would continue to be part of my "new" life. One obvious indication of my background was my accent. Colonels Jager and Admiral Deutermann were the models for me as I chose a school based on its R.O.T.C. program. These were men whose duties appealed to me and seemed to have worthwhile careers. But when it came to enrolling at Syracuse University, a connection forged all the way back in Split turned out to be important.

When I started at Syracuse, Ivan Meštrovic was in his fifth year as a professor of art at the university. His ties to my family and influence within the university were factors in my decision to attend Syracuse. People unfamiliar with sculpture may not know of Meštrovic's fame or significance. I myself was not aware of all that he had endured and accomplished. I did know, however, that Syracuse was a place with a friendly face from my hometown of Split.

Meštrovic was born in 1883 in Vrpolle, Croatia. He apprenticed with a stonecutter in the Dalmatian hinterlands and acquired the skills of a master sculptor. By the time he was 22, he had his first show, held in Vienna. In 1908 he moved to Paris and began to acquire international fame, especially as the foremost twentieth-century sculptor of religious subjects. He was the first living artist to have a one-man show at the

Ivan Meštrovic

Metropolitan Museum of Art. Prior to World War I, he moved back to Croatia, but the war forced him out of his homeland. For two decades, Meštrovic was forced to live in various European cities thanks to the continent's divisive politics. During World War II while he was in Yugoslavia the Ustashi imprisoned him for three months. For the rest of the war, he lived in Switzerland, Rome, and Paris for different periods.

In the 1930s, a relatively calm period in Yugoslavian history, he purchased land and built a villa in Split, which was next door to the bank and building my father had purchased as a weekend getaway.

The family became friendly with him and family during the summer months when Meštrovic resided in Split. His contacts with us actually went back farther than being neighbors during the summer. He was a close friend of my mother's brother, who was no longer living when I was born. Consequently, my mother had known Meštrovic during the years when as boys he and my deceased uncle had become best friends.

After World War II, when Meštrovic was living in Paris, the chancellor of Syracuse University, William Pearson Tolley, met the sculptor and was deeply impressed. Tolley had come to Syracuse in 1942 (and remained until 1969), and was keen on expanding the school's campus and national influence. Tolley was responsible for bringing R.O.T.C. to Syracuse, and also for establishing a fine arts sculpture program that achieved national prominence. Tolley saw in Meštrovic an artist who could raise the university's profile in the fine arts. He promised the Croatian a studio and planned to make Meštrovic an important figure in the university's growth.

Our family's friend, whom I visited many times during my studies at Syracuse, stayed at the university until 1955, the year that I also left with my undergraduate degree. He went to another academic position close to the often Roman Catholic subjects of his religiously inspired sculpture — the University of Notre Dame. But during his time at Syracuse, Meštrovic's fame increased. The American Academy of Arts and Letters in 1953 awarded him the organization's Gold Medal for sculpture. In 1954, Meštrovic became a United States citizen. So prominent was the sculptor by this time that the nation's president, Dwight D. Eisenhower, presided over the ceremonies.

When I was at Syracuse, I visited his studio about once a month. Later in life, my wife and I helped my alma mater construct a sculpture garden to commemorate his work and contribution to Syracuse University. During the 1950s, my interests were not in the fine arts. I had other responsibilities and pursuits to keep me busy. But even if Meštrovic's art was peripheral to my experience as an undergraduate student, his identity as a native of Yugoslavia was not. As much as I desired to be an American and serve in the nation's military, my own European background continued to inform who I was and what I would become even as an American citizen.

CHAPTER 38

Auditing R.O.T.C.

The Reserve Officers' Training Corps (R.O.T.C.) is a college-based, officer commissioning program, designed as a college elective that focuses on leadership development, problem solving, strategic planning, economics, and professional ethics. Its origins go back to the Civil War. In 1862, with the Morrill Grant, which established such notable land-grant colleges as Michigan State University and Pennsylvania State University, the United States Congress stipulated that institutions receiving the grant would provide instruction in agricultural and technical subjects. The federal program also required that land grant institutions include instruction in military tactics. Over time, the United States military established training programs for prospective officers first at its own military colleges and eventually at participating civilian institutions such as Syracuse. R.O.T.C. programs still produced significant leadership within the American armed forces. Colin Powell, for instance, former chairman of the Joint Chiefs of Staff, was an R.O.T.C. participant at the City College of New York about the same era in which I was involved at Syracuse. During the 1960s, many of these programs at non-military colleges came under attack from faculty and students who objected to the Vietnam War. But in the 1950s, almost no one doubted the value of R.O.T.C. programs. Popular support for the military and for the American efforts to combat Communism remained strong.

To join the R.O.T.C. programs, I needed to be a citizen of the United States. Just as my family and I had to wait for our number to come up before we could acquire visas to reside in America, so I was required to wait the stipulated five years before becoming an American citizen. Technically, the earliest I could qualify for citizenship was December 24, 1954, the five year anniversary of my disembarking at Ellis Island. This also meant that according to the rules of the different branches of the military, I could not participate in an R.O.T.C. program until the second semester of my junior year at Syracuse. Because it was a four year course of training, it seemed impossible for me to join one of the R.O.T.C. programs. In fact, the Navy and Army turned me down.

At first, the Air Force R.O.T.C. program also denied my request. How can a non-American legitimately qualify to be an American soldier, let alone an officer? But I persisted and a sergeant agreed to hear my case. When I explained my background, my intentions, and my willingness to be part of the Air Force R.O.T.C. without receiving the stipend (including salaries) or perks that went to its members, he agreed to talk to his boss, the officer responsible for the Syracuse chapter, Colonel William M. Holleran. Colonel Holleran was a highly decorated veteran pilot of World War II who would go on to distinguished service, after retiring from the military, as the top civilian at the National Security Agency.

Holleran was impressed by my story and likely talked to other Air Force officials who recognized that my European pedigree and language skills could be useful for the United States' new conflict with Soviet Communism. The agreement the U.S. Air Force R.O.T.C. made with me was that I would need to audit all of their courses; I could not receive any financial remuneration; and I would even need to purchase my own uniform. Holleran also told me that if I did well in the courses, and qualified to become a citizen, he would be glad to attend my swearing in as a U.S. citizen. This was just one more instance of great encouragement shown to me by one of America's military officers. From this perspective, I could never understand why the nation or the servicemen who fought its wars came under such fierce criticism during the 1960s and the Vietnam War. I could not fathom why the protesters and critics did not also realize how the United States had countered and defeated genuine tyranny in Europe, was continuing to fight another form of oppression in Soviet Communism, or opened amazing opportunities for the likes of immigrants like my family and me.

Becoming an officer was not the only path into the military in those days and many American young men took the alternative route. They enlisted and went off to fight in Korea without training first to be an officer. I actually seriously contemplated that path.

So in addition to my regular courses at the university, some of which seemed to contradict what the U.S. Air Force R.O.T.C. was trying to teach us, I buckled down and studied hard in what was my unofficial major at Syracuse.

CHAPTER 39

Entrepreneurial Skills

Although I was only auditing my R.O.T.C. classes, I also had more at stake in those courses than the men enrolled in the regular program. If I did not excel, the sergeant and Colonel Hollerman would have reason to sever my tenuous connection to their unit of prospective officers. I felt that I had no room for error. If I were going to be selected for the final stage of officer training, I needed to master all the material. I did. I received good grades in all my R.O.T.C. courses. I did well enough also to pass all of my other courses, though I must admit that economics drove me crazy with all of its theory and seemingly no practical know-how. I earned high marks in geography and chemistry. Geography may have come naturally to me because of my own wayfaring background. Chemistry had no real appeal and I saw no use for it. But again, I was very good at memorizing formulas, which was all I needed to pass the required chemistry courses with flying colors. At the same time, I had a singleness of mind about serving in the military that made my R.O.T.C. courses a priority.

In addition to my regular course work, I was a member of the Psi Upsilon Fraternity. I worked as many as four jobs to support myself — and even then my dad, who was not exactly prosperous at this point, was sending me three dollars a month to help with my expenses as a university student. One of my jobs was waiting tables at the Tri Delta sorority. This provided pocket money which allowed me to date some of the coeds whom I served on the job. I also obtained a job stocking the furnace daily with coal at the Psi Upsilon Fraternity. At the time, it was the wealthiest fraternity at the university and I was one of Syracuse's poorest students. For that reason, it was an unlikely development when one of the fraternity's members, my future brother-in-law (more in the next chapter), encouraged me to pledge at Psi Upsilon. At the time, fraternities were generally civilized and my future frat brother required nothing for membership from me that caused embarrassment. It is the fifth oldest fraternity in the United States and originated in 1833 in New York State at Union College. In 1837 when one of Psi Upsilon's brothers at Union transferred to New York University, he started another chapter, which began the fraternity's history of expansion. Psi Upsilon came to Syracuse in 1875.

In addition to waiting tables and stoking the furnace at the fraternity, I also bought a vending machine business from one of my fraternity brothers for $50. I paid him in installments. He did not think the candy and cigarette machines were very lucrative — he considered stocking them more of a nuisance than anything. But for me the routine of scheduling vendors, stocking the machines, and collecting profits was simple. And it paid surprisingly very well. At one point I was netting $50 per week, a fortune. Granted, this line of work meant that I received my salary in lots of nickels, dimes, quarters and half-dollars. When I went out on dates, I would pay the check not in one- or five-dollar bills but from my stash of coins. These were not as valuable as those coins I carried around during my days in Italy. But those gold coins had prepared me well to handle non-paper forms of currency. During my senior year, my success also allowed me to buy a car, which was a big deal to me because of how much owning an automobile had been part of my family's status back in Split. Granted, I could not afford car insurance, which was not mandatory in those days. If years later my own children had purchased cars without insurance, I would have put an end to the car. But even if this car was in bad shape — the brakes were shot — and uninsured, I had acquired one of the most important emblems of independence for average Americans.

Despite all the work and studies, I became an active member of the fraternity and participated in all their events.

The odd jobs I took while a university student extended to my summers. Back in New York City, I discovered my knack for sales. At first I went out on my own, going door-to-door at fancy apartment houses. I would tip the front-doorman to let me circulate within the building. I started by selling women's leather pocket books. I purchased them from my brother-in-law's brother who was in the leather business in Brazil. These purses cost me between $3 or $5, depending on the size, and I sold them for $20 or more. Although I was good at this, I soon tired of the hustle. So I took a job at Saks Fifth Avenue. I was drawn to the lavish interior of the building and its merchandise. One of my first successes at Saks was selling toy guns that were headed for the discount stores unless someone could sell them. I wound up selling all of them. When the manager asked how I did I it, I told him that showing the toys to boys and talking directly to them prompted the boys to plead with their mothers to make a purchase. I later transferred to a different department and again had great success selling underwear and pajamas. Simply being pleasant to customers and talking about the value of the product was key. The store's manager wanted to hire me as department head. This was my first shot at a business career, but I was still intent on becoming an Air Force officer and never gave the job offer a second thought.

Another summer I took the skills I had learned as a page at Irving Trust and applied them to truck delivery. I lived with my brother Paul in Troy, New York at his fraternity at Rensselaer Polytechnic Institute and took a job delivering frozen foods for a local distributor. One day would be devoted to loading the truck, then hooking it up to the power supply overnight to keep the freezer working and the food cold, and then delivering the truck's contents the next day. These were big trucks, requiring an eight-gear transmission for the engine. I could never use more than six gears, but since most of my deliveries were local, my inexperience with the transmission was no problem. Only when I delivered to Grossinger's Resort Hotel in the Catskill Mountains — over a two hundred mile round trip — were my truck driving skills tested.

Otherwise, I excelled in my duties as a deliveryman truck driver. I usually finished a load in two-to-three hours. My favorite stop was a local nunnery; this was a great advantage since the nuns were fond of me and fed me well. I must have still looked like a immigrant in need of a good meal. The nuns asked for two deliveries each week instead of the normal allotment of one per week. This way they could feed me twice. I loved their meals and was grateful for their help.

Since I was not busy during all of my nine-hour shift, I asked my boss for more stops. He obliged at first but then the shop steward of the local union heard about my industriousness, and challenged me to follow protocol. First, he insisted that I join the union, or else. "Or else" was loud and clear. I did join the union and for a brief time was a member of the Teamsters during the infamous era of Jimmy Hoffa, Sr. Next, the foreman told me to slow down. He said, in fact, that delivering more than my allotted produce in less time than a normal shift was "not allowed." Thanks to the pace of union work I was directed to acquire overtime and for the summer I averaged three dollars per hour (including overtime). The steward laced his threats with mocking remarks about my accent. At one point he even spoke to me about slowing down while holding a baseball bat in his hand. This was not the America I thought I knew. I was much more accustomed to the energy and productivity of immigrants who needed to earn a buck.

And earn bucks I did that summer in ways beyond food distribution. Paul and I opened a bar in the basement of the fraternity where we were living for the summer. For a few days we sold beer at a great mark-up. We had no idea that state laws regulated the sale of alcohol. We had not experienced Prohibition. Once we realized our oversight, we closed down the operation, with regret.

Another summer I found a job on weekends at the country club where Paul worked. I was a lifeguard and a waiter. Sometimes the customers in the restaurant and bar could be a real nuisance. One time when a foursome on the golf course had arranged for a round of vodka martinis to be brought to them when they reached one of the holes farthest from the club house. I caught the assignment and after the bartender mixed the drinks, I delivered them on foot to the golfers. After settling with the customers and realizing they had left me a tip of a nickel I was not in the best of spirits. That experience as a waiter would leave a lasting impression and to this day, I over-tip wait staff. But for the most part, the other customers were very generous. That summer, working at the country club, I cleared over $1,500, which today would be the equivalent of more than $12,000 (a fortune). I may not have grown up in the United States, but I had acquired the nation's work ethic. I didn't believe in handouts then and I still don't, except in cases where people are incapable of working.

I did not reflect on my work experience much at the time, but I was acquiring sufficient skills to be a success as a civilian. However, I was young, idealistic, and wanted to work off my debt to the United States and its armed forces. What better way to do it than by becoming an officer and defend the country.

America —
Land of the Free. Home of the Brave.

CHAPTER 40

Fraternity Brother and His Sorority Sister

The adage about all work and no play making Jack a dull boy did not apply to my experience as a Syracuse University student. I loved the courses in the R.O.T.C. program and thoroughly enjoyed my work in its various forms. Simply being on the campus of an American university, after what I had experienced for the first eighteen years of my life, was plenty exciting. But I appreciated female companionship and dated periodically in rare spare time. As a waiter at several of the sororities, I came into regular contact with Syracuse's coeds, some of whom seemed to be charmed by my accent and Slavic features. I recall that I had as many dates as I wanted, or more likely, for which I had free time.

Dating assumed a more important part of my activities after one of my fraternity brothers introduced me to his sister. Larry Baner was one of my house mates at Psi Upsilon and had been a great help in securing a spot for me in the fraternity. He later transferred to Dickinson College but while he was at Syracuse, he was one of the students in my closest circle of friends. My best friend during college was Robert Evans, who was also connected to the Baners and would eventually marry one of Larry's sisters. One of Larry's other sisters, Phebe, had attended a party at the fraternity with another one of the brothers. I was there as a waiter. Phebe noticed me and commented favorably to her brother, Larry. He initially told her to forget about me because, in his view, I did not speak enough English. But that did not stop her or me from eventually going out and becoming regular companions.

Although I was basically the same age as Phebe she was two years ahead of me in school. She had enrolled when she was only sixteen. I had lost time during the war so that I did not start at Syracuse until I was nineteen. What helped to negotiate any potential awkwardness

Phebe Baner and Mike Novakovic at the
Syracuse University R.O.T.C. Ball, 1953

for an underclassman dating a senior was that once Phebe graduated, she remained in the area, taught in the Syracuse public schools, and attended graduate school at the university.

Another factor that helped build our relationship was the proximity of Phebe's father, who was pastor at First United Methodist Church in Syracuse. Before coming to Syracuse in 1949 he had been the Superintendent of the Methodist district in Southern New Jersey and pastor of a congregation outside Camden. First Methodist Church was one of the largest congregations in the city and his sermons were broadcast every Sunday on the local radio station. Soon after the family's relocation to Syracuse, Dr. Baner's wife, Phebe Sharp Baner, died after a prolonged battle with a brain tumor. Single-parenting at the time was unusual. Dr. Baner himself had experienced the loss of his mother as a boy and then, by his father's decision, was reared by one of his aunts. He was not going to let his own children, one boy and three girls, experience the double loss and be forced to leave home. In addition to his pastoral outlook, as a single parent he was particularly attentive to the needs of others and saw I was among the neediest at Syracuse. He and I had a very strong relationship based on mutual respect and trust. On one occasion when I was visiting Phebe in the Baner home, he noticed me making soup and thought that I was not eating properly. He told Phebe then that she should bring me to his home (where Phebe was also living) regularly for good, home-cooked meals. After my history with hunger, Phebe didn't have to do any arm-twisting.

My relationship with Dr. Baner was one of the most encouraging I established while at Syracuse. Instead of inspecting me for my potential as a spouse for his daughter, he was an amazing source of support. It did help my cause that I was a hard worker. He also approved of my participation in the R.O.T.C. program, which showed that I had some of the virtues necessary to be an officer and actually even a gentleman. Although I had not been a soldier during the war — I did witness combat and was more like the veterans enrolled at Syracuse on the G.I. Bill than the average American college student. For the former G.I.s and me, the college atmosphere of sports and parties was less appealing than the serious business of getting training for life beyond the degree. I am sure that Dr. Baner also noticed this about me.

When Phebe's and my relationship progressed, and her father went to New York City to visit with his prospective in-laws, my parents, his fondness for me only seemed to increase. The tragedies that he had experienced as a boy and as an adult formed a natural bond with me. Of course, this was still the 1950s and no one was talking about themselves as victims. Phebe's and my parents' generations did not talk openly about hardships. Neither did we as border-line members of the so-called "greatest generation." But even if we did not speak about these troubles, we did sense them and knew as kindred spirits those who had suffered great loss.

Once Phebe and I met, my time at Syracuse was pretty well fixed. Although we would not be married until I finished my degree, we were seldom apart for the last two years of my undergraduate education. We loved each other's company and started a life-long romance that was grounded in the highest possible respect and care. I had few worries about how to occupy my time. Between studies, jobs, and Phebe, my schedule was full.

CHAPTER 41

From Immigrant to Citizen

My legal status in the United States as a senior at Syracuse University was filled with anomalies. I wore the uniform of Air Force R.O.T.C. students but was not officially a member of the group. I was also intent on serving in the military but was still not a citizen. I was learning to speak the national language well but still had a Serbo-Croatian accent. Plus, on campus I belonged to the most prestigious fraternity at Syracuse but had to work hard just to pay for my tuition, food, and clothes. I was in effect still living like an immigrant even while engaged in some of the most American activities — going to college and training to be a military officer.

Technically, I was an alien. That was how the Immigration and Nationality Act (INA) of 1952 (also known as the McCarran-Walter Act) classified someone in my position. This legislation was a response both to the unprecedented immigration of displaced persons after World War II and the lack of a uniform national policy for naturalization. Before the INA's implementation, a variety of statutes governed immigration law but were not codified within a single text of federal policy. (Since the attacks of 9/11, INA's provisions have been revised beyond the changes in 1965 which abrogated the quota system that restricted the number of immigrants from certain countries.) INA defined three types of immigrants — those with special skills or with relatives in the United States, ordinary immigrants whose rate of acceptance was not to exceed 270,000 per year, and refugees. On the side of greater inclusion, the Act reduced a number of racial restrictions that existed in previous iterations of policy. On the other side of the coin the Act codified suspicions of immigrants engaged in subversive activity, especially Communists, and established provisions for deporting such persons. INA instituted what has now become the norm for all immigrants. It stipulated that before applying for citizenship, an alien must be at least eighteen years old and must have been lawfully admitted to live permanently in the United States. Aliens needed to have resided in the United States for five years and, for the last six months, in the state where he or she sought to be naturalized. Applicants also needed to be of good moral character and "attached to the principles of the Constitution." INA also supplied examples of persons who did not measure up morally — drunkards, adulterers, polygamists, gamblers, those who had lied to the Immigration and Naturalization Service, murderers, or anyone imprisoned for more than 180 days during residence in the United States.

As definite as this law may have sounded, it also contained wiggle room. For instance, in some cases the number of years for residency prior to naturalization could be cut from five to three years. INA also contained provisions for aliens who had served in the United States military during World War I, World War II, or the Korean War. According to Act 329, "no period of residence or specified period of physical presence within the United States or any State or district of the Service in the United States shall be required" of the people who had engaged in such military service. At the same time, as much as Congress may have attempted to give coherence to a seemingly baroque process, the lawmakers who crafted and wrote this law could not enforce it.

As it turned out, my application for citizenship advanced along two paths, both the military route and the one paved by personal connections. In the former case, my work in the R.O.T.C. impressed U.S. Air

Force officers and they looked for ways to apply the stipulations of INA to my application and they did.

The New York State Supreme Court justice swore me in as a citizen, on March 12, 1955 at the state court in Syracuse, I was in effect also entering the United States Air Force. The oath that I took was required of all naturalized persons, according to Act 337 of INA:

(1) to support the Constitution of the United States;

(2) to renounce and abjure absolutely and entirely all allegiance and

fidelity to any foreign prince, potentate, state, or sovereignty of whom or which the applicant was before a subject or citizen;

(3) to support and defend the Constitution and the laws of the United States against all enemies, foreign and domestic;

(4) to bear true faith and allegiance to the same; and

(5) (A) to bear arms on behalf of the United States when required by the law, or

(B) to perform service in the Armed Forces of the United States when required by the law, or

(C) to perform work of national importance under civilian direction when required by the law.

Not specified in the oath, but also required of everyone who took it was that each person be "of good moral character, attached to the principles of the Constitution of the United States, and well disposed to the good order and happiness of the United States." I certainly was attached to the principles of the Constitution and especially committed to the good order and happiness of the United States. I took this oath with tremendous pride, honor, devotion and commitment. ***I SWORE TO SACRIFICE MY LIFE TO SUPPORT THE CONSTITUTION.*** I never forgot my obligations, and live by those principles.

America —
Land of the Free. Home of the Brave.

Part Three
An Officer and a Gentleman

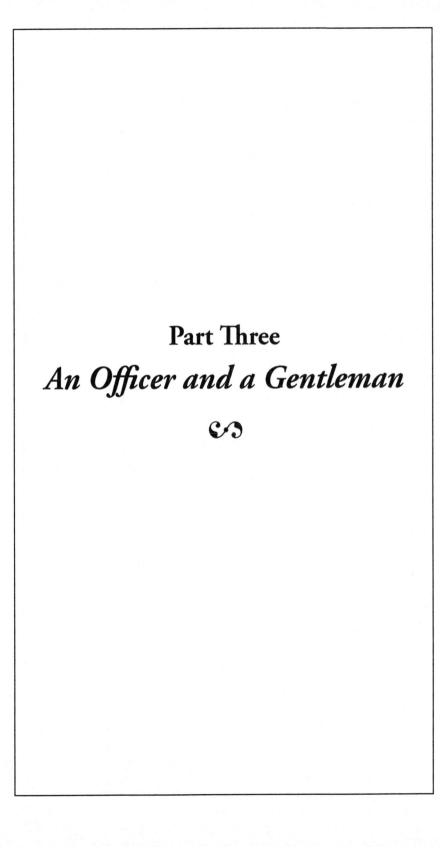

CHAPTER 42

Graduation

O ur commencement speaker at Syracuse University was Averell Harriman, then the Democratic governor of New York State, originally a banker, then an advisor to FDR and Truman, and a man with presidential ambitions.

Most of the details of the ceremonies at Syracuse's 1955 commencement have faded from my memory, partly the result of their routine nature but also owing to the training I still had ahead of me. I do recall that my parents did not attend. They were still not in a position to make the trip from New York City. My status as a United States citizen, along with my completion of the R.O.T.C. course at Syracuse, meant that I was only beginning my training for the Air Force. Consequently, soon after I had picked up my diploma and turned in my cap and gown, I was ready for basic training.

My instruction as a soldier would not come immediately, so I filled my time in Syracuse with what I enjoyed most — working, plus continuing to court Phebe. One of the odd jobs I found was to work with a Canadian carpenter, Eric Thresh, who was a member of the Methodist church and had served in the United States Army. I needed income and he was looking for an assistant, so he took me on and taught me basic carpentry skills. Our strategy that summer was to drive around the city and look for homes with porches. For those that looked like they needed work, we approached the owner or resident and gave a bid. Our rates were cheap compared to other carpenters but for us, as young men the money was great. I could not work long for Eric, but we began a life-long friendship. He went on to be recognized as a highly successful business entrepreneur. There were no handouts.

Finally my orders came on February 6, 1956. I was soon headed for basic training at the Lackland Air Force Base in Texas. Since the Korean War had ended a couple of years earlier, the Air Force had no specific plans for me. Still, I needed to undergo the training required of all American soldiers in the Air Force.

Basic training involved learning routine field exercises, weapons training, classroom instruction in war skills, lessons in field security, and physical fitness. During my time at Lackland, as you might expect, the military was stressing lessons learned during the Korean War. This involved putting trainees through a small bivouac, called "Little Korea," in which we were exposed to real gunfire. Another innovation during this time of training was practical field training that prepared us for work at a functioning air force base in a conflict zone. At Lackland this meant constructing unique encampment area behind the base hospital (later Wilford Hall), that resembled an air base in Korea, where we lived and trained "in the field" — so to speak — for the better part of a month. I was on hand for a significant new initiative with the inception of a two-phase training program for male trainees. In the first phase, we went through the paces at Lackland and then transferred to the base's technical training school for five more weeks. What I remember most was the physical training, the obstacle course, and especially the maze of underground tunnels into which they would drop us and then leave us to find our way out. Some of the trainees spent the better part of a day trying to see daylight. I was able to find a route back to fresh air after little more than an hour.

Another innovation that was hardly path breaking but still meaning-ful occurred during my time at Lackland. Texas at that time of year was very hot. I was familiar with warmer climates having grown up in Split and spending time in Italy, but this heat was unbearable at times. Basic training by its very nature was rigorous: we ran everywhere — to the latrine, to the cafeteria, to class, and also to the course where we ran as part of our physical training. A welcome relief came then when we enjoyed a break and were permitted to see a movie.

Overall, the time at Lackland was uneventful. I waited to hear about my next assignment.

I was thrilled to graduate from basic training in Texas, although we had no notable civilian to give us advice about what to do with the rest of our lives. I was still under the command of R.O.T.C. officers in New York State and needed to report there as soon as training finished. A couple of my friends and I decided we would see part of the country and drive from Texas to New York. On our first stop for an overnight rest at a small town in Alabama, we discovered that none of the motel owners would give our African-American friend access to a room. This was a real surprise since all of my time in the United States had been in New York where racial prejudice existed but formal or legal expressions of segregation were much harder to see. We decided to make the drive all the way to New York City by swapping driving responsibilities and sleeping when not behind the wheel. We made the trip — which wound up being good training for some of the exhausting hours I experienced in the Air Force — in thirty-eight hours.

That experience in the South was a significant one in my understanding of the United States. I had encountered no hostility from Americans because of my accent or my background of being from a "Communist" country. I soon learned, as well, that the military would be remarkably welcoming to me, though part of that greeting owed to the various languages I spoke. The United States military clearly knew how to take advantage of its recruits and officers' backgrounds. Still, the military also led the way in breaking down the barriers of segregation. After

President Truman's executive order in 1948 which called for integration throughout the military, the armed services started to implement the new policy. From that point forward, integration of the United States military became standard procedure. And that certainly dovetailed with my own experience of the United States and my time in the military. For many African-Americans the fastest way to becoming a "regular" American was to serve in the military. The place of minorities in the military did reinforce my perceptions of American soldiers from my childhood. They were fair, generous, and decent. That was the kind of military I believed I had joined, and it was the kind of nation for which I was willing to fight.

CHAPTER 43

To Fly or Not

So far my training for the Air Force had included practically everything except flying. The importance of aerial warfare had been crucial to success in two world wars. In 1947, the U.S. Air Force became a separate branch of the American military, carved out from responsibilities formerly held by the Army. During World War II, the United States Army Air Corps (USAAC) functioned with great autonomy but only after the war did the Air Force achieve formal independence. This meant that the command structure and procedures of the Air Force were taking shape almost at the same time that I was becoming an officer. Hierarchy and policies aside, I still needed to learn to fly if I were going to be part of the Air Force.

Soon after returning to Syracuse, I received orders to go to flight school in Florida at Bartow Air Force Base just outside of Orlando. Used off and on by the military during the early 1940s, after World War II, Bartow became a municipal airport to serve the small surrounding community and its barracks were converted into apartments for returning G.I.s. But by 1950, with the demands of the Korean War and increasing hostilities between the Soviet Union and the United States, the federal government reactivated it again as an Air Force base used primarily to train student pilots. It served as a U.S. Air Force primary flight training facility for the Air Training Command (ATC) from 1951 to 1960. During this time its 3303rd Pilot Training Group trained both commissioned U.S. Air Force officers and U.S. Air Force aviation cadets. More than 8,000 men graduated from primary flight training at Bartow, among them Colonel Edwin E. "Buzz" Aldrin, Jr., who trained there in 1951. He went on to a distinguished career in the Air Force and piloted Apollo 11, the first manned lunar landing in history.

The aircraft in which I first trained was the Civilian Piper Club and then the T-6 "Texan," which flew under a number of names depending on the military using it. Designed and produced in 1935 by North American Aviation, the T-6 was a single-engine advanced trainer aircraft. It was used almost exclusively for flight training initially by the United States Army Air Forces, United States Navy, Royal Air Force and other air forces of the British Commonwealth. During World War II and into the 1950s, the T-6 was known by a variety of designations depending on the model and operating air force. The U.S. Air Force designated it as the "AT-6," the U.S. Navy the "SJN," and the British Commonwealth air forces, the "Harvard." Only during the Korean War was the T-6 pressed into service as forward air control aircraft, used to insure that bombing raids struck the right targets. It was a popular training plane because its features were so simple. Many pilots would later say that learning to fly on the T-6 was as easy as driving a car. The only real complication came when having to rely on radio instruction to land the plane.

Flight training proved attractive for the structure, discipline, and camaraderie. I admired the men at flight school for their commitment. My fellow trainees noticed my accent and would ask about my background. I soon became one of the favorite storytellers as I recounted my family's experiences in Yugoslavia and Italy during the war. I must have told the story so often that eventually the details of my life came to the commander's attention. My knowledge of Eastern Europe and my fluency in several languages made me an obvious candidate for intelligence. Officers from Washington soon came to Florida to interview me about my background. They also sent me to a psychologist who conducted a series of tests to see if I had the makeup to go into intelligence. I passed those rigorous exams, not the first in my training as an intelligence officer, and soon the officers from Washington asked me to go to a special intelligence school for the armed forces outside the nation's capital and elsewhere. After very extensive training, I had found my place in the United States military. It was in intelligence.

Mike at Flight School, 1956
Bartow Air Force Base
just outside of Orlando, FL

CHAPTER 44

All Expense-Paid Honeymoon

From flight training school and an initial round of intelligence training at different facilities, I returned to my home, which was still New York City, the place where my parents and sister lived. Phebe was still teaching school and attending graduate school in Syracuse. By this point in our romance, I had proposed, she had accepted, and her father gave his blessing.

Phebe and I had planned to marry in the fall of 1956, which was almost six months after I returned from intelligence school. But my papers came through in the spring of 1956, which assigned me to the intelligence unit in Frankfurt, Germany. So instead of marrying in the fall, Phebe and I needed to move up the wedding date. Arranging with the minister (Phebe's Dad) and finding a church was no problem. My best man was Robert Evans and the matron of honor was his wife, Jenny, Phebe's sister. And, we still had our big wedding.

We had wanted to go to Canada for our honeymoon by way of Niagara Falls. We got to Niagara Falls but then had to leave and report to Manhattan Beach. In the military, we would live on a very tight budget throughout my early career since salaries, even for officers, prior to an all volunteer military, were meager. At least we had a place to stay (back at Manhattan Beach AFB) and we knew that our honeymoon would be a fourteen-day "cruise" to Europe all expenses paid by the Air

Force. What was unclear was how much time we could spend together during our honeymoon. I was one of several officers on board a Liberty Ship, sailing from the port of New York to Bremerhaven, Germany. We left New York on July 17, 1956.

This trip was not what travel agents would have advised for newlyweds. Liberty Ships were bare-bones cargo vessels, ordered during World War II in response to the critical need for these ships. Eighteen different ship builders constructed over 2,700 Liberty Ships between 1941 and 1945. Their design failed to generate good reviews from the public. *Time* magazine called the Liberty Ship an "ugly duckling," and FDR, despite his own orders for production, referred to the design as a "dreadful looking object." But, they got the job done and at least 2,400 Liberty Ships survived the war. The military used some in a variety of functions while Greek and Italian shipping lines bought others.

Meanwhile, I was a new husband and needed to think about Phebe. She was an incredibly good sport about it all. We actually had to be out of our rooms every morning at 7:00 am for the cleaning personnel. Phebe struck up a friendship with the ship's commanding officer's wife, who taught her how to play bridge, which she did most days while I attended either to the business of ship logistics or instructions about my assignment in Germany.

The trip turned out to be useful preparation for our life together while I served as an intelligence officer in the Air Force. I could not tell Phebe about my work. She needed to find outlets for socializing and friendship. Neither of us complained. We were delighted to be together, thankful for and honored by the opportunity to serve our nation, and curious to see what post-war Europe was like.

CHAPTER 45

Monitoring the Soviets

I went to work in Frankfurt as a second lieutenant, part of an office euphemistically called the Historical Research Unit. The second word was accurate since our task was to conduct a lot of investigation. But our studies were only remotely historical. Our assignment specifically was to gather human intelligence that would allow the United States to follow the movements and plans of the Soviet Union's military.

One important source of information was the movement of people of German origin back into Germany, either by agreement or force, following World War II. The number of people returning to Germany from Poland, Czechoslovakia, and even from East Germany was overwhelming. Our work was relatively simple. We would go to the Central Station (rail) and wait for persons of German descent to disembark. We then interviewed them to see what they could tell us about life in the Soviet-controlled Communist countries from where they had come. My German was good and I had no trouble deciphering all manner of accents and dialects that came our way. I also had native fluency in Serbian, Croatian and Italian, a working knowledge of Polish, and was studying Russian.

One of the people I interviewed was an engineer who came to West Germany voluntarily. He was escaping from the Communists. He told me from first-hand knowledge that the Soviets had designed and built a submarine that could go as deep as 1,500 feet below sea level, a figure that was unprecedented at the time. This number was so dramatic that when I reported this to my superiors and Naval intelligence, the response was disbelief. But within a year, the U.S. Navy submarine units confirmed this intelligence. United States military strategists needed to calculate their operations in response to this new capability of Soviet submarines. I was elated to have my report verified. This incident taught me the importance of searching for new Soviet warfare developments. It was a good lesson which I never forgot.

Our unit started with about three dozen Americans and about the same number of others, mostly from German backgrounds, who like me had sought refuge in the United States and West Germany. Our task was not simply to find out about life on the other side of the emerging Iron Curtain, but also to look for Soviet spies. We may have had better intelligence-gathering equipment at the time than the Russians, but they had numbers on their side. And they used the policies governing the repatriation of displaced persons to flood West Germany with German spies and needed to return to their native land. Some of those returning had been part of German military units and had defected to Russia at the end of World War II.

Mike receiving Commendation Medal of all Air Force
intelligence operations in Europe from Colonel Opper

When we found someone who was loyal to the Russians, we had little power to detain them. Plus, the laws governing refugees at the time meant that they needed to reside in West Germany. So we attempted to persuade them of the superiority of political freedom in western societies and our democratic form of government. Having firsthand experience with Communist Partisans during my childhood and adolescence, I could also speak plausibly about the advantages of the United States and the ideals for which it stood. All of us in the office knew that we had a much better story to tell than the Soviets did.

Another significant piece of information about Soviet technological advances I secured came through an interview with a person of German descent who came to Germany by way of western Russia. He had read in a small newspaper published in one of the towns in the Ural Mountains that the Soviets had developed a rocket system and had launched its first spacecraft, *Sputnik*, which entered outer space on October 4, 1957. This was a shocking development that eventually forced the United States to counter with its own space program. But when I initially reported this to my superiors, and they relayed the intelligence to Washington, the response was again one of disbelief. I was stubborn and persisted with the report and eventually the State Department and military leaders in the United States acknowledged the news. Thanks partially to that report, I was promoted to Captain and given responsibility for a staff of approximately thirty officers and non-commissioned officers. My new office was in the old IG Farben building, the huge German company which the Allied forces broke up into separate smaller companies, many of which are still thriving to this day — Bayer and BASF among them. The Nazis had used this office during the war. It was the nicest office I had for a long time. It was large and with oriental rugs on the walls, but I never forgot it had once been home to a great evil.

Among the major events that occurred during this tour of duty was the Hungarian Revolution. International politics complicated the situation and prevented the West from intervening, as many in my office thought we could end it. One complicating factor was the Egyptian decision to nationalize the Suez Canal. The French, British, and Israelis responded by bombing Cairo. As Vice President Richard Nixon would later explain, "We couldn't on the one hand, complain about the Soviets intervening in Hungary and, on the other hand, approve of the British and the French picking that particular time to intervene against Nasser."

That was a good lesson for me. And it was also a good education for me about the inner workings of military and political affairs. As I watched the United States help to defeat evil during World War II, I had been inspired to join that effort. I went to Frankfurt, keen to set the world on fire with the United States' ideals of freedom, liberty and equality before the law. I soon realized that promoting freedom and democracy required brains and finesse as much as brawn.

Colonel Opper, Phebe and Mike. Mike received
the 1959 Award for U.S.A.F. Intelligence Missions.

CHAPTER 46

Family Life of Intelligence Officers

My unit in Frankfurt was part of the new foreign military presence in the recently created Federal Republic of Germany. The Allied powers that defeated the Nazis divided the country west of the Oder-Neisse line into four occupation zones for administrative purposes during 1945–1949. In the western part of Germany, the United States, Britain, and France each had distinct areas of governance. The Soviets oversaw the east. The United States zone consisted of Bavaria and Hesse in Southern Germany, and the northern portions of the present-day German state of Baden-Württemberg. In addition, the United States was responsible for the ports of Bremen and Bremerhaven in order to have access to portions of Northern Germany.

The hope originally was to govern Germany through the Allied Control Council, a body that functioned for about two years. Its responsibilities ran from the significant issues of demilitarization and denazification to the trivial matters of telephone tariffs and treatment of venereal diseases. The Council broke down thanks to growing tensions between the West and the Soviets. All along, each of the occupying powers held authority in their own districts but the Council was an expression of a desire for a unified Germany and international goodwill. In the western zones, cooperation continued and by 1949 the American, French and British sectors merged to form the Federal Republic of

Germany. That left East Germany to the Communists and it became the German Democratic Republic, a misnomer that I always found ironic. Tyranny is still cruelty no matter what you name it.

Just before I arrived, the Allied forces devolved complete control to indigenous German authorities. In May of 1955, the German Treaty went into force. It ended West Germany's status as an occupied territory and granted the rights of a sovereign state, with certain restrictions that remained in place until German reunification. At that point, the British, French, and the United States high commissioners were replaced by formal ambassadors from each country.

During the time of occupation, strict rules were in force that regulated the interaction between the Allies' personnel and the Germans. Part of this caution stemmed from a desire to protect the Allies from ongoing security threats from the German population. Some leaders also wanted to avoid offending the native people.

When Phebe and I arrived in Frankfurt the rules governing fraternization were no longer in play but we faced our own set of barriers thanks to my work in military intelligence. An even more basic obstacle to our life in Frankfurt was the difficulty we had finding living quarters. Housing was at a premium in post-war Germany. We found space on the third floor of a private home. We had no hot water in the apartment, and only a one burner stove. We shared a bath with the German family from whom we rented. To take a bath, we not only needed to find a time when the bathroom was free, but we had to allow two hours for the hot water heater to heat enough water for a bath. I could take showers at the officers' club. Throughout most of my military career, Phebe taught elementary education. It helped stretch an Air Force officer's meager salary.

Our living situation was difficult, and we were newlyweds, but the idealism of early marriage helped us cope. We thoroughly enjoyed living in West Germany. We were also lucky since so many soldiers in Europe were deployed without their wives or children. Plus, the cost of living was low. We could go out for a very good meal for one dollar a person at some of the best restaurants in the city. Movies were a dime. Gasoline cost only twenty cents a gallon. In addition, the German people, despite the ambivalence of the occupying forces, were very hospitable. They sometimes seem demoralized because of their defeat. But they offered no resistance and showed no signs of resentment.

Some of the best times in Frankfurt were with the other officers in my unit and their wives. Because the rules governing intelligence officers forbade socializing as large groups in public places, we usually crammed into one of our small civilian apartments for meals and bridge. Eventually, we got government housing — former SS officers' quarters. In our own apartment, we lacked enough chairs to handle a big crowd so guests would sit on the floor, even to eat a meal. The sense of purpose we shared was an important ingredient in our fraternizing. Also, the past from which many of the intelligence officers had come was another bond among the officers and their spouses. One Thanksgiving dinner that we hosted, Phebe told me something I had not noticed. She was the only American-born in the group. Many of the other officers and their wives were, like me, from Eastern Europe and had sought safe haven in the United States after World War II. Some of the women had been in deportation camps and several of the men had taken circuitous routes to escape war-torn Europe and find freedom across the Atlantic. All of us were volunteers, devoted to a common mission and to the United States and each other. The stories of the war those fellow officers and women told were remarkable. This shared background made our times together all the more inspiring.

CHAPTER 47

World Events Intervene Again

The final year of our time in Europe was the hardest for us personally. We had moved to Milano, with our two-year old daughter, Phebe, where I was working entirely undercover. (I am still unable to reveal the nature or scope of my assignment.) Phebe was completely isolated since I was "flying solo" and not connected to an intelligence unit. She spoke little Italian at first. Fortunately, she's a fast learner. But we also had no telephone in our apartment, and no television. The only radio programs available were in Italian or on Armed Forces Radio. She did not know where I was when I traveled, which was often, and if an emergency came up she was completely on her own. In the event of an emergency, she had a telephone number she would call in Rome.

One of those emergencies turned out to be a blessing in disguise. A few months after our arrival, our daughter developed a high fever and Phebe went out to look for a physician. She spoke enough Italian by then for the locals to take her down the street to the neighborhood's practitioner. She rushed with him back to our apartment. All the while he was assuming Phebe was German because we had moved from Frankfurt. But in the apartment Phebe called out to our daughter in her native tongue — English — to try to comfort the little girl. When the doctor heard my wife's English, he responded in kind. He explained that he had studied medicine for two years in the United States while working in a New York City hospital emergency room. That man, Dr. Venicio Picolli, became a friend. We traveled together in Europe and he later visited us in the United States.

Eventually, we returned to the United States and orders sent us to Travis AFB in California. A small community near the base, Vacaville, was where we found housing. It was also the location of a California state prison. We rented our apartment from the superintendent of the prison. Phebe and I heard lots of stories about prison life and California politics. I had plenty of time to hear these stories because my assignment at Travis was primarily a time for me to recover from my tour of service in Frankfurt and Italy. I did have responsibilities monitoring flight paths and managing the maps that were necessary to Strategic Air Command's (SAC) war plans.

Since I was familiar with the world of intelligence, I thought about a career in the Federal Bureau of Investigation (FBI). And to enjoy responsibilities in the agency commensurate with my experience, I figured that I needed to go to law school. Consequently, I applied to Dickinson Law School in Carlisle, Pennsylvania where Phebe had relatives and where my parents were then living. My father loved the small town feel of the historic college town. Each day he dressed in coat and tie before walking downtown where he would find a cup of coffee and read the newspapers. It was not exactly the café culture of Europe, but my parents made many friends in Carlisle. Once accepted at Dickinson, I decided to change my status into the Air Force Reserves.

But war and international conflict, which I had known practically my entire adult life, would again intervene and change my life and that of my family. During the summer of 1961 when Phebe and I, along with our daughter Phebe, were settling down in Carlisle, Pennsylvania, we turned on the television on July 25th to watch a nationally broadcast speech by President John F. Kennedy. He was going to address the recent escalation of hostilities between the western members of the former Allies (England, France, and the United States) and the Soviet

Union in Germany. We heard the President reiterate that the United States was not looking for a fight with the Soviet Union and that American officials were aware of the "Soviet Union's historical concerns about their security in central and eastern Europe." He spoke of his willingness to renew talks with Premier Khrushchev regarding the division between East and West Germany. But in addition to signaling a desire to avoid armed conflict, Kennedy announced that he was going to ask Congress for an additional $3.25 billion for military spending, mainly on conventional weapons. Kennedy also indicated that he wanted to see the creation of six new divisions for the Army and two for the Marines. To meet this demand, he planned to triple the figures for drafting citizens into the military, and call up the reserves. The capstone of the speech was the line, *"We seek peace, but we shall not surrender,"* a very appropriate statement today. Kennedy also called for an increase in the Army's total authorized strength from 875,000 to approximately 1 million men, along with an increase in the active duty of the Navy and Air Force from 29,000 and 63,000. This had the feeling of the beginning of another war in Europe.

The president's speech came mid-way during a period of the Cold War known as the Berlin Crisis, which ran from June 4 to November 9, 1961. This was the last major politico-military European incident of the Cold War. It stemmed directly from the Soviets' post-World War II expansion throughout eastern and central Europe and the complications that ensued in the German capital of Berlin from the West's presence in Germany. The Soviets had instigated the crisis by demanding the withdrawal of western armed forces from West Berlin. That ultimatum prompted a professional crisis for me and my family — whether to remain in law school or return to full-time active duty in the Air Force. At this time we were also delighted that our family had increased in size. Our son Michael Branko was born. It was wonderful to have all the relatives around to share in our joy.

But, in light of events in the world, I wanted to reconsider my decision to go to law school and pursue a civilian career. Would I continue with plans to attend Dickinson or go back to active full-time service with intelligence? But the decision was made for me. I was recalled. Since I felt an obligation to the United States, and Phebe shared my desire to serve the country when called upon, I readily and gladly went back. I had not forgotten that I had sworn allegiance to defend our country. Within three days I was gone. When I said so long to Phebe, I also reassured her that I would return in a week. It turned out to be several months before I came home.

Going back into full-time service in this case meant taking an assignment with the Eighth Reconnaissance Group at Westover Air Force Base in Springfield, Massachusetts. I worked directly on Strategic Air Command war plans during the Berlin Crisis, while waiting to be deployed to Europe.

CHAPTER 48

A Civilian Intelligence Officer?

During my first tour in Frankfurt I knew that the Soviets were not content with the lines drawn in Germany at the Potsdam Conference. But none of us thought they would go as far as to construct a wall through the city of Berlin to prevent the movement of Germans from the Communist controlled sector of Berlin to the West.

After World War II, many of those living in the Eastern Bloc countries aspired to enjoy the freedoms available to residents and citizens of Western Europe. The migration of people from Soviet-occupied countries to the West between 1945 and 1950 prompted many Eastern Europeans to apply for political asylum in West Germany. The applications in 1950 totaled 197,000, in 1951 165,000, 182,000 a year later, and all the way up to 331,000 in 1953. In response to this movement of people and their desire for greater political freedom, the Soviets constructed a barbed-wire fence between East and West Germany in 1952. But Berlin was available to civilians as a point of exit, especially for East Germans. The city was still under the rule of the four-joint occupying powers, England, France, the United States, and the Soviet Union. Some Eastern Bloc citizens who found a way to Berlin could possibly escape to the West through the loophole the city provided owing to provisions for Germany under the Potsdam agreements. But in 1955, the Soviets once again reneged on these Potsdam provisions and passed a law under which they became the exclusive guardian of civilian movement through Berlin. The last straw, apparently, was the 1956 determination by East Germany to eliminate all travel between the East and the West, even so-called visits by East Germans in the Federal Republic of Germany. Some East Germans had used these visiting papers to defect altogether. By 1961, 3.5 million East Germans had left for the West, which was twenty percent of East Germany's population. The brain power loss was significant. Engineers, physicians, teachers, lawyers and skilled workers left the East. Part of my work in Frankfurt between 1956 and 1959 was to interview these defectors. We learned much about the conditions behind the Iron Curtain, but none knew about the Soviets' or East Germans' plans to stop the population flow. The primary purpose of the debriefings was to see if the Soviets were preparing for a sneak attack. After all, the invasion of Czechoslovakia was supposed to be only an "exercise." Since it turned into an occupation, we did not want another exercise to take an additional part of Europe into the orbit of Soviet-dominated governments.

If Berlin was a crisis for Communists in the East, it soon blossomed into a crisis for the West. To stop defectors to the West, the Soviets tried to gain control of the entire city. In 1958, they issued an ultimatum to their former Allies that Berlin should become completely independent and free from all military presence. When the Western powers refused to comply, the English, French, Americans, and Soviets agreed to meet in 1959 at a conference. Three months of meetings produced no resolution but did lead to Nikita Khrushchev's two-day summit with President Dwight Eisenhower at Camp David the same year. After that visit the President said, "There was nothing more inadvisable in this situation than to talk about ultimatums, since both sides knew very well what would happen if an ultimatum were to be implemented." What both sides seemed to think would happen was war. Now the stakes or chances of armed conflict were higher because of the prevalence of nuclear weapons on both sides. Khrushchev had a habit of increasing worries about a confrontation thanks to his public performances, such as the one he gave a year later at the United Nations when he objected to the speech by the Philippine ambassador, by pounding his shoe on the delegate desk in protest. The Soviet Premier objected to the patently correct charge that the Soviets had swallowed up Eastern Europe and deprived the population of "the free exercise of their civil and political rights."

By 1960, the time of a presidential election and the end of the Eisenhower administration, the situation in Berlin had escalated into a full-blown crisis. A summit to address Berlin scheduled for May of 1960 to be held in Paris, again with all the Allies participating, came to naught because of the famous U-2 spy plane incident in which a United States aircraft piloted by Gary Powers was shot down over Soviet air space. After initially denying the intelligence purpose of Power's mission, the United States conceded that the plane was part of its surveillance of the Soviet Union, an admission that caused the country embarrassment in the run up to the Paris Summit. The conveners were forced to cancel the summit.

The situation in Berlin now fell to the Kennedy administration. Khrushchev immediately tested the new president on June 1, 1961 by issuing an ultimatum when he signed a separate peace treaty with East Germany that would end the existing four-power agreements guaran-

teeing American, British, and French access rights to East Berlin. This treaty, according to Khrushchev, would go into effect unilaterally on December 31, 1961. Two weeks later, Walter Ulbricht, the president of East Germany, who had already advised

Construction of the Berlin Wall, 1961

Khrushchev about the need for force to stop defectors, said in a press conference that his government had no plans to erect a wall. This was, of course, a piece of disinformation because two months later Ulbricht signed an order to erect the Berlin Wall. It was eventually more than eighty-seven miles long and included a second fence 100 meters into East Germany, the construction of which required the demolition of all the homes along the wall. This area, called a "Death Strip," was covered with raked sand or gravel to allow easy detection of footprints. Initially the wall was only a barbed-wire fence. From 1962 to 1965, it became a reinforced wire fence. Finally, in 1965 it took the form of a real concrete wall, and in 1975 a border wall.

These developments made me eager to be deployed. During the worst of tensions, while I was at Westover, everyone was armed and ready to "go." This meant being armed and ready to be deployed in case of a Soviet attack, including the cooks. I actually traveled to Berlin from Westover for a couple of missions to help develop strategic plans in the event of war. Instead, a showdown between United States and Soviet tanks in Berlin during October of 1961 did not lead to open warfare but resulted in a standoff. Although both sides were under orders to shoot if fired upon, and General Lucius Clay, the United States commanding officer in Berlin, was prepared to use the American tanks to bulldoze the wall, neither side moved its tanks aggressively or fired a shot. Instead, the Kennedy administration determined that Berlin was not of vital interest to the United States and agreed to live with the wall, a decision that many strategists and foreign policy analysts later lamented.

During my time at Westover, I revisited my plan of serving in domestic intelligence under the auspices of the Federal Bureau of Investigation, with law school as the necessary route to a higher level of responsibility within the Bureau. I also considered the CIA but after initial conversations with recruiters, concluded that they would likely send me back to Europe. I did not want to leave the United States military only to be reassigned to Europe by civilian intelligence authorities.

I had already applied to the FBI while at Dickinson. Since World War I, special agents under the Department of Justice and the Attorney General were responsible for policing illegal interstate commerce — such as prostitution and, during Prohibition, alcohol — with some attention to espionage and acts of sabotage. With the rise of communism and related Red Scares in the United States, more of these agents' duties were directed to domestic cases of espionage. By the time of the FBI's formal start in 1935, intelligence gathering assumed a large proportion of its responsibilities. For instance, in 1939 and again in 1943, President Roosevelt authorized the FBI to carry out investigations of threats to national security. Presidents Truman and Eisenhower further defined and expanded these powers such that any public or private agency or individual with information about subversive activities was urged to give the information to the FBI. In 1946 the Bureau's authority expanded when it received direction to conduct background investigations on government employees. The Atomic Energy Act of 1946 also gave the FBI the task of determining the loyalty of individuals with access to restricted information about atomic energy. These were the sorts of activities that made my background in military intelligence and gathering information on Communism a natural fit within the FBI.

But during the 1950s and early 1960s, the work of the Bureau shifted away from domestic cases of espionage and back to policing the kind of gangster activities that had originally prompted the Department of Justice to employ a special force of agents. Congress passed new federal laws against racketeering, gambling and civil rights violations and empowered the Bureau to enforce such legislation. Consequently, as I was settling on the idea of working in civilian intelligence, the FBI was assuming more responsibilities that made my experience less useful than it would have been a decade earlier.

I sensed this change first hand as I went through the battery of interviews for a job in the Bureau. The process took me all the way to a face-to-face meeting with William C. Sullivan, the third-ranking official in the FBI behind J. Edgar Hoover and the only liberal Democrat to break into the top ranks of the Bureau during Hoover's tenure. He had started with the FBI during World War II when Hoover dispatched him on an undercover intelligence mission to Spain. By 1960, he was directing the FBI's domestic intelligence division. My meeting with Sullivan was exceptionally intriguing but I will not go into details except to say that they made me a good offer.

CHAPTER 49

"Peace Is Our Profession"

Those were the words that greeted me when I first drove on to the Westover Air Force Base, just outside of Springfield, Massachusetts, the next stage of my military career, and the longest time for my wife, children, and me to live on a military base. We stayed there about two years. It was an easy transition from law school back to full-time in the Air Force since I was already familiar with the operations at Westover, thanks to my deployment during the height of the Berlin Crisis. It was great to be there with my family. When John F. Kennedy visited the base on October 23, 1963, I was able to take little Phebe with me. She witnessed the president very well from her perch on my shoulders. We were only a few feet away from the president but because Phebe was up so high she almost touched him.

Westover was originally known as the Northeast Air Station when constructed in 1940 as part of the Army Air Corps. During World War II it functioned as a training site for bomber and fighter crews. After the war, it served as a point from which to transport equipment and personnel. Finally, in 1955 it assumed the functions that took me there: SAC assumed control of Westover and the base became the home for operations of the 405th Air Refueling Wing and the headquarters for the Eighth Air Force, which moved from the Carswell Air Force Base in Fort Worth, Texas. A year later the 99th Bombardment Wing also used Westover as its base of operations. I was there as part of an SAC technical reconnaissance unit responsible for establishing and monitoring targets in the Soviet Union.

SAC was both a Major Command of the United States Air Force and a "specified command" of the United States Department of Defense. SAC operated the United States' land-based strategic bomber aircraft and intercontinental ballistic missile (ICBM) strategic nuclear arsenal. SAC also oversaw the logistical infrastructure necessary to support bomber and ICBM operations, including refueling bombers in flight, as well as running strategic reconnaissance missions, flying command post aircraft, and at the beginning even supplying fighter escorts. In effect, the simple but comprehensive mission of SAC was to provide long-range bombing capabilities anywhere in the world.

Within the command structure of SAC itself some of the greatest initiatives of the time were logistical. During the 1950s, under the leadership of then-Lieutenant General Curtis LeMay, SAC became instrumental in developing jet engine aircraft. In order to provide atomic-armed long-ranged bombers for the purpose of defending the U.S.A. in the event of war, the Air Force needed new aircraft. At the beginning of the decade, for instance, SAC had only sixty aircraft which could deliver nuclear weapons, and none of these had the long-range capabilities that war and defense strategy dictated. By the end of the decade the jet-engined B-52 became the backbone of SAC, accounting for over half of its aircraft and eighty percent of its bombers.

The greatest liability of all jet aircraft was their limited range. But the other breakthrough in SAC logistics at the time was the process of in-air refueling.

While SAC took the lead in supplying the tools for nuclear war, the United States' civilian administrations took responsibility for war policy. Harry S. Truman, the only president to sanction the use of nuclear weapons, gave little attention to the ways in which to integrate these bombs and missiles into a larger pattern of defense and war strategy.

For him, nuclear bombs were a "big stick" of last resort to threaten antagonists. For Dwight D. Eisenhower, a man with great military experience, nuclear weapons were part of a larger strategic policy, both to deter the Soviets and to comfort allies. Under his administration, John Foster Dulles, the Secretary of State and the Pentagon developed a Single Integrated Operation Plan (SIOP) which called for launching numerous nuclear weapons at the Soviet Union and other parts of communist Asia. There was concern about the Soviets' capabilities during the early stages of the Cold War. But the United States wanted the Soviets to know that if they attacked America first, the consequences would be devastating.

CHAPTER 50

An Officer and Especially a Gentleman

Toward the end of my assignment at Westover, I learned of a possibility of returning to Europe for another tour of duty. To go back to Europe, however, I needed additional intelligence training. So in the summer of 1965, Phebe and I packed up the family and headed to Lowry Air Force Base in Denver, Colorado to receive further instruction on intelligence gathering.

In Denver I attended classes in the morning from 6:00 to noon, and then study during the afternoon. On my way home on October 22, 1965, I stopped to pick up some milk and bread for the family. As I was driving to the market, I saw a young man attacking a woman at the Hoffman Heights Shopping Center in Aurora. I did not have any idea about the reason for the attack. I only knew that this man was going to hurt this woman seriously if she did not get away. Other people were around and were watching the incident. But none came to the woman's defense. So I yelled at him, and told him to stop. Once he realized that someone was going to challenge him, he grabbed her purse took off running.

I got out of the car and chased him. Initially, I caught him and dragged him down to the street. But this young man was a tough guy and he got up and continued to flee. This was one of the first times in my life when I encountered someone faster than I. Since he was ten years or so younger than I was, and since I was in uniform, he got away fairly easily.

I returned to my car and pursued him with the aid of an internal combustion engine. Once this fellow saw that I was no longer running after him, and that I had gotten back into the car, he assumed that I had given up. But I finally found him after driving around the area. He was walking across the local high school football field. I did not want to see him get away again, so I drove my car on to the field. Once he saw the car, he started to run again. I continued to pursue in the car and even thought about trying to knock him down with the vehicle. Eventually, though, he tripped and fell and this gave me another opportunity to catch him.

By this time the attacker was tired but he made up for it in size. We fought in that football field for several minutes and I received more than I gave. The man hit me hard in the nose. I fell to the ground and it looked like he would get away again.

But driving by at that time was a man in a pick-up truck who saw the fight and decided to see what was going on. He ran over to us during the fight and was carrying a rifle. Once it was clear that I was not going to be able to subdue the attacker on my own, the driver snuck up behind my opponent and hit him in the head with the butt of his rifle. It turned out that the driver was the local deputy sheriff. He had been out hunting. His return was as fortuitous as his shot gun was effective. The sheriff arrested the attacker.

For my efforts in coming to the assistance of the lady, I received the Air Force's equivalent of the Army Soldier's Medal. This Airman's Medal is awarded to service members who, while serving in any capacity with the U.S. forces, distinguish themselves by highly commendable actions, usually at the risk of life, but not involving actual combat. The report written by the Navy Lieutenant which contained the recommendation for the award stated that I had "demonstrated . . . extreme bravery by taking the initiative to assist the victim of the attack and robbery, commencing a determined chase to apprehend the attacker and to physically subdue the man." The recommendation mentioned my physical injuries for which I received treatment at the base's dispensary. It even documented that my blue Air Force uniform had been ripped during the incident.

My own sense was that it was not a big deal.

CHAPTER 51

Return to Germany

Fresh from my training in Colorado, in 1965 we went back to Europe, arriving with my family just in time for Christmas. By this point in my military service, I had resolved to stay in the Air Force. I even had aspirations to become a senior officer. The way to do that involved "punching your ticket" at different stops in the Air Force's missions and activities. Some of this included going to the right schools that opened possibilities of service. Advancement up the chain of ranks also required working in different theaters of operation. When I had previously served in Germany, I was assigned to human intelligence — interviewing refugees and immigrants coming from Eastern Europe and Soviet Bloc countries. This time I was returning with my recent training — collecting intelligence from various methods of communication, written and electronic. It also meant going to a different city. This time it was Wiesbaden, Germany.

After World War II, the Wiesbaden Airfield became the headquarters for the United States Air Force in Europe. The Germans had originally built the facility before the war as part of the Luftwaffe's base of operations. The Germans abandoned the facility in 1945 and United States forces took it over. During the initial friction between the Soviet Union and the Western Allies, the airfield in Wiesbaden served as the base of the United States Air Force flights throughout Europe. But as the conflict deepened and Cold War strategy depended on both side's capacity to deliver nuclear weapons to vital targets, Wiesbaden became impractical as the home to squadrons of United States bombers. It was too close to East Germany and too vulnerable to a Soviet attack. Even so, the Air Force continued to use Wiesbaden as the forward based headquarters — the command center closest to front lines.

My own intelligence work was only indirectly related to the deployment of aircraft, whether on reconnaissance or bombing missions. Phebe and I could live off the base and we decided to do so. One reason was that we went back to Europe with two small children: Phebe, who was going into third grade, and Mike, who was still a toddler. We wanted to expose the children to the German way of living and chose the small village of Oberjoshbach. It was tiny, with some 300 villagers, but a lovely place in the mountains outside Wiesbaden.

We also grew to love the people there, partly through the school where our daughter, Phebe, studied, but also through our domestic help. We enrolled Phebe in the German school during the summer months. She learned to speak perfect German. She also had classes on the local flora and fauna in the mountains that took the students out to the trails. The Germans wanted girls to acquire domestic skills so Phebe started to learn to knit and sew. She became especially adept at the multiplication tables because, in the German system if you did not know the equations, you would be forced to sit under your desk. In the United States students only sat under their desks as part of an air raid drill.

We also became acquainted with a wonderful woman, Frau Graff, who offered her services to us as a domestic assistant. The townspeople warned us about her because of her husband's reputation — he was alleged to be some sort of criminal. But she was an amazingly hard worker — cleaning carpets according to the German standard of taking them out and beating them free of dirt. She was also a good friend to our daughter. When the town was preparing for its annual religious parade to honor its saint, she, being childless, asked if Phebe could accompany her because you needed a child to participate. We agreed and bought Phebe the white dress worn by all girls in the parade. This gave Frau Graff one of the only chances to walk in the town's parade. After the parade she took Phebe back to her home for cookies and cider. It was a lovely time for us and our daughter.

But once my wife took a job with the American school teaching second grade, we decided to move into the quarters for American officers in Wiesbaden. We regretted leaving Oberjoshbach but the commute for Phebe would have been too long. Plus, this gave her more time to be with Mike, Jr.

My work was classified, and provided the U.S.A. with tactical as well as strategic information. I received a letter of commendation from Dr. Roy S. Cline who later became head of the CIA.

Towards the end of my tour of duty, word came that I would be receiving orders for Vietnam. I was sent for temporary duty to Oberammergau for combat training. We left Wiesbaden in the summer of 1969. After helping Phebe move back to Syracuse, NY, I received orders and left for Vietnam. Now the burden of rearing the children and maintaining the home fell entirely on her.

One more time Phebe showed her intellect and guts.

CHAPTER 52

Vietnam and the Limits of Intelligence

By the time I arrived in Saigon on August 13, 1969, fighting Communism had defined my service in Air Force intelligence. Even before becoming an officer in the United States armed forces I had firsthand experience with Communists both in Yugoslavia and in Italy. As bad as the Fascists were, my family and I also knew that Communist Partisans were just as bad — and often worse. My tours in Europe, first during the 1950s and then during the middle of the 1960s, had involved indirect confrontation with the Soviets. The United States had declined to engage the Soviets when they expanded into Hungary and Czechoslovakia but the overarching Cold War strategy by America and NATO was to contain Soviet expansionism. Operations in Europe in which I participated, consequently, involved using intelligence, both by human observation and technological surveillance, to monitor Soviet strategy and deployments. It also included determining appropriate targets for a response to Soviet aggression, calculating risks, and making recommendations to civilians responsible for developing United States defense plans and foreign policy.

My year of service in Vietnam, which lasted from 1969 to 1970, exposed me to a new set of responsibilities in the context of direct conflict with Communist guerilla forces. As in Korea, where geographical divisions along the lines of Soviet and American influence proved sufficiently unstable to prevent war, the division of Vietnam after World War II geographically along northern and southern lines was designed to rid the country of aggressors from WWII (the Japanese) while recognizing the historic powers in the region. This meant restoring the French to their colonial interests in the South, and ceding the North to the Chinese who were supposed to be non-Communist. But when indigenous movements for independence in the North, led by the Communist Ho Chi Minh, ran up against French plans to expand their rule into North Vietnam, war was inevitable. In addition to the emerging resistance in the Third World to European colonialism, the conflict in Vietnam, begun as early as 1946, also emerged as a real front in the Cold War between the free West and the Communist East.

Once the French left Vietnam in 1954, the international powers determined to divide the country in two, with the North and South as distinct sectors and each determining its own rulers through free and open elections. This was also the time that the United States began to send special advisors to South Vietnam, partly under the influence of John Foster Dulles' Domino-theory which held that once one government fell to Communism in a region, surrounding governments would also fall. The elections in the North and the South did not materialize, but instead, governments emerged that were either decidedly Communist (North Vietnam) or anti-Communist (South Vietnam). The South Vietnamese government was by no means a model of liberty or democracy but because of its anti-Communist doctrine it received significant support from the United States. In 1961, when John F. Kennedy became president, the United States had 1,600 special advisors in South Vietnam who were responsible for training the local military on how to fight the guerilla forces of the Viet Cong. By 1963, the number of American special advisors had risen to 16,000.

After the Gulf of Tonkin incident in August 1964, when North Vietnamese gunboats attacked two United States destroyers that were sailing in international waters, the Senate authorized President Lyndon

Baines Johnson to use war powers to assist any country seeking to preserve its freedom. American troops landed in Vietnam the following
year and the campaign of bombing North Vietnam began. From 1965
to 1969, the United States invested heavily in the Vietnam War, sending as many as 500,000 soldiers, many of whom were drafted. The war
was unpopular in the United States, partly from campus-wide protests
at university and college campuses like my alma mater, Syracuse, and
from the images shown on nightly television news broadcasts that were
biased against the United States' involvement in the war. Vietnam was
the first televised war and the footage and photographs did little to
build support for a war where the United States' interests were not obvious to the wider public. It was also one of the first wars where United
States soldiers experienced the limitations of conventional military
operations. Our soldiers had received training to fight along the lines
of lessons learned in World War II and Korea. But they were up against
soldiers who used guerilla tactics, most of whom did not wear uniforms,
and easily blended in with the civilian population in South Vietnam.

When I arrived in Vietnam, the work of military intelligence was
already under assault, though few Americans knew about it at the time.
Within the Johnson administration and Pentagon, policy analysts, such
as Daniel Ellsberg, leaked information damaging to American forces.
He had already objected to the intelligence that the Senate used to justify the escalation of the war after the Gulf of Tonkin incident. In 1971,
The New York Times released the "Pentagon Papers," documents that
Ellsberg had surreptitiously obtained to expose the American military's
behavior during the early stages of the Vietnam War. The intelligence
community, both military and civilian, lost credibility with the wider
public. But those doubts had already started before Ellsberg allowed the
Times to publish the "Pentagon Papers." In January of 1968, the North
Vietnamese launched the Tet Sheepshead Bay Offensive, a so-called surprise attack on South Vietnam, hoping to end popular support for the
war in the United States. This assault seemed to surprise the Johnson
administration and Pentagon.

In retrospect, that string of conflicts in late January and early February of 1968 was actually a victory for United States military which inflicted very significant losses on the North Vietnamese. It had also been a victory for parts of the military intelligence forces. The losses suffered by the Air Force, for instance, were minor because of precautions taken through the acquisition of field intelligence about the deployment of North Vietnamese and Viet Cong forces. Some branches of the military, those who suffered the most in the Tet Offensive, refused to believe these intelligence reports, and neither did Defense Secretary Robert S. McNamara. But the difficulties of that war and the inability of the White House and the Pentagon to manage public perceptions of Vietnam turned what should have been a symbol of the United States' superior strategy and military personnel into a sign of the nation's weakness. Ho Chi Minh had lost a high percentage of his human (and logistic) assets in South Vietnam. He knew the Tet Offensive was a major loss, but we knew it too. Jane Fonda and her ill-informed and naive protests encouraged Ho Chi Minh. He decided he could survive because of the loss of support in parts of the United States.

This was the situation when I arrived in Saigon to assist in running the human intelligence gathering operations Detachment 6, 6499th Special Activities Group at the Tan Son Nhut Air Base for the entire theater of operation.

USAF Security Service patch   *Special Operations Logo*

CHAPTER 53

The Intelligence of
Montagnards and Rhodes Scholars

The intelligence effort in Vietnam was complex. The objective was to find and follow military, paramilitary, logistical and political organizations of the North Vietnamese in South Vietnam. This extended to locating enemy forces, logistical supplies, base areas, sanctuaries, trails, roads and rivers located in Cambodia and Laos. The U.S. was also concerned about access to air space and to the waterways within the Mekong Delta which provided the enemy with pathways to logistical support and reinforcements. We also needed to monitor the quantity and quality of war materials being supplied by China and the Soviet Union and its satellites to the North Vietnamese. The United States Army coordinated the intelligence activities of all Army, Navy, Air Force, and Marine Corps efforts. In 1965, Americans had 320 officers and soldiers engaged in intelligence gathering. By 1969 that number had increased to over 3,000.

I came to Vietnam as a Major, but with Lieutenant Colonel's responsibilities for day-to-day operations. My rank mattered little since I wore plain clothes more than my uniform. I was responsible for six teams of intelligence personnel, including hand-picked South Vietnamese officers and senior NCOs throughout the country — Da Nang, Pleiku, Nha Trang, Saigon, Phu Quoc, and Cu Chi. Saigon was the headquarters. When I needed soldiers who had been trained to fight in the jungle, I usually worked with the Marines on special operations, responsible G.I.s in my experience. My duties took me throughout South Vietnam to each of these different locations. I also had ties to intelligence gathering in Cambodia that required travel there. Sometimes to receive communications I needed to leave Vietnam and the region altogether and meet agents in Hong Kong, Singapore, or elsewhere. On one of my trips to Singapore, British officials detained me and even conducted a strip search. Sometimes spies needed to spy on other spies, even if we were on the same side. I was happy that our methods of carrying secret information could not be found by those invasive methods. My suspicion is that my accent made them think I was not a United States officer.

My responsibilities meant that I had over 100 military personnel reporting to me, including agents in other parts of southeast Asia. I had a strong staff with many bright and dedicated people. Three of them were Air Force Academy graduates — two of whom were Rhodes Scholars, one of whom became an ambassador. The other was a scholar of French who wound up teaching at the Air Force Academy for much of his career.

The native Vietnamese with whom I worked and had direct daily contact were also very impressive. The Montagnards — the French word for "people of the mountains" or "mountain dwellers" — were a group ethnically distinct from the rest of the Vietnamese and had a troubled relationship with the government in the South. During the 1950s, for instance, South Vietnam's president, Ngo Dinh Diem, attempted to indoctrinate the Montagnards with Vietnamese culture. This increased their desire for autonomy and even a separate nation. It also made some of the Montagnards sympathetic to recruitment of the North Vietnamese Communists. But during the 1960s, the South Vietnamese allowed United States Special Forces to contact the Montagnards and train them to fight and keep tabs on the North Vietnamese. During the war, as many as 100,000 Montagnards served in some capacity for the U.S. military. These people also suffered for their loyalty to the United States. As many as 200,000 (almost twenty percent) of Montagnards lost their lives, including half of the adult male population. After the war, thousands fled to Cambodia seeking refuge. The United States eventually assisted the resettlement of many Montagnards to North Carolina.

My own experience with the Montagnards was memorable. I made many trips to the Pleiku region during my tour to solidify our already strong relationship with the natives, but two visits stand out. My first trip took me to the hut of a Montagnard chief who wanted to cooperate with the United States military but demanded confirmation through direct contact with a senior officer. Although the chief ruled over a village of about 1,000, organized according to family clans, he lived in a small hut no bigger than the average American suburban bedroom. When I entered, he was sitting on the floor with his seven wives, all of whom were bare chested, only wearing skirts made of grass. To ritualize the visit, the chief had arranged for a meal of Montagnard delicacies. I was expecting monkey, since that was the advice I had received from fellow officers back in Saigon. The custom was to bring a live monkey into the room, cut open its head and serve its brains straight from its cranium. I am not sure that even the hunger I had experienced in Italy could get me to eat monkey brains. But instead of monkey the chief had ordered fried bats. These were very large rodents with wingspans between five and ten inches. Of course, to be polite and to insure the services of the chief and his tribe, I needed to eat. The bats tasted like rotten chicken and had a putrid odor. I was relieved not to have been served monkey brains. But the thought of eating bat was no better. My strategy was to nibble at the bat to make it look like I was eating. And then, since I was wearing combat fatigues with numerous pockets up and down the pants legs, I would slip the rest of the bat meat into one of the pockets. The technique worked. I did not offend the chief and he agreed to work with us. He remained loyal to the United States military.

Death was the reason for another visit with the mountain people. A funeral arranged for one of their tribal leaders — a grandmother of the chief — required the presence of a senior officer. I was glad to go because of my admiration for the chief who openly wept during the ceremony. The funeral was simple, touching and painful at the same time. It was also long. It started with a period of drum beating in which the mourners walked around the hut where the dead body lay. All of the natives wailed and sobbed during the death march. They also chanted words that I could not understand. Finally, after what seemed like hours of chanting, they stopped and kissed each other before burning the body.

Of all the dead bodies I saw over the course of my life, this was the strangest, even stranger than seeing Mussolini hanging by his feet in a square in Milano. The fight with Communism had taken me a long way, to places and people I could not have imagined when I was a boy in Italy.

CHAPTER 54

Combat

When I was in flight school back in the 1950s, what impressed me about the life of an officer was its structure and routine. I enjoyed the chains of command, daily schedules, and clearly defined responsibilities. When I arrived in Vietnam, though, the days were not routine or orderly. The reasons stemmed partly from the nature of intelligence work but also from the character of the Vietnam War itself.

When I arrived, I was a Major with a direct reporting line to General George Sykes. The officer directly above me was Colonel Mike Bellovine, a good-hearted, fair, and aggressive Colonel, and one of the first Jewish-Americans to go to West Point. He was a great leader. At the time, the Viet Cong had a price on the heads of some intelligence officers.

I lived as did the officers who reported to me, but this was not because we were remote from the fighting. I was stationed at the Tan Son Nhut Air Base in Saigon, where I had access to as many helicopters as my unit or I needed, an office, and my room in the barracks. But my responsibilities took me all over Vietnam, Phu Quoc Island, and into Cambodia. The actual combat was infrequent.

Some of the fighting I experienced was similar to what I had grown up with — bombs and missiles sent by the enemy either at the air base in Saigon or at different compounds outside the city and outposts. What was markedly different from Italy was that now I could do something in response to the attacks other than simply bearing them and hoping not to be hit. Sometimes the nighttime sky would light up over the base from explosions and from the numerous flares to assist locating the enemy.

As a boy, I could hear planes coming before they dropped their bombs — even if I was asleep. As an officer, I could not sleep through skirmishes. On one occasion during a confrontation in the jungle I would need to sleep to stay clear headed. And during those times, I learned to sleep right next to a six-inch howitzer, even while the three soldiers responsible for loading and firing it, shot the enemy. Those fire support bases were extraordinarily effective. The sound of those guns discharging ammunition, however, may be responsible for some of my current loss of hearing.

A couple of times I was simply an object of a random attack by the Viet Cong. On one of my trips by jeep from the northern part of South Vietnam down to the south, the soldiers with me stopped to eat.

Mike in helicopter, Vietnam

We pulled up by the side of the road and unseen enemy soldiers shot multiple rounds at us. We ran for cover but never saw the attackers. We then finished our C-rations and left.

Another attack came during one of my helicopter trips into the jungles of South Vietnam. As our aircraft was landing, our unit came under a barrage of rifle fire, again from enemy soldiers whom we could not see. In our haste to find cover I jumped out of the helicopter earlier and higher than I should have and injured my back. I did not immediately feel the injury, but it has lingered through my life and now needs therapy injections to manage the pain.

Sometimes the fighting was the direct result of my own confrontations with the enemy. Intelligence received by my unit indicated that the enemy might have been using a radar tower at the southern tip of South Vietnam, on the Cambodian side, to monitor the flight patterns of United States aircraft. I needed to find out if this tower was in fact a radar unit. But I did not like sending my men out on a mission with which I myself had no experience. So I requested a unit of new troops, and we headed out in jeeps to check the tower. Unfortunately, these new soldiers had not been trained well about the nature of jungle warfare and headed out as a group, walking together en masse. I had to show them that they needed to spread out, walking abreast, twenty feet apart, both to avoid being an easy target and to be able to inspect more territory. We were taking sufficient hostile fire for me to question the value of going all the way to the tower. So I instructed the men to regroup and get out of the area. I had the coordinates of the tower and ordered it destroyed by air strike.

Part of my unit's combat involved decisions on other targets, though this was not the kind of planning I had participated in at Westover. For example, one of the most gruesome scenes I witnessed was the devastation by a Viet Cong raid on a Navy field hospital in Nha Trang. The guerrillas snuck in one night from the sea with explosives and rigged them to go off once they had left. Then they returned that evening and killed any of the patients and medical staff who were still alive. Our policy was not to retaliate by striking a North Vietnamese hospital. It was against the Geneva Convention. But their placement of enemy hospitals next to air bases or military installations also hurt our ability to select targets that would not result in the deaths of hospitalized North Vietnamese and their wounded. This was the sort of pressure we were under.

On the whole my work in Vietnam was varied and hectic with almost no structure. I traveled constantly throughout the country by jeep, helicopter, and especially the Air America flights that ran as a shuttle service between Da Nang, Saigon, and other areas. On one of these flights I had a disturbing experience. I was in a hurry and needed to return to Saigon. I saw a plane, a C-130 Cargo aircraft, was in line to take off, contacted the pilot directly and asked him if I could board the aircraft. He told me that I would probably want to wait for the next plane. But the situation was urgent, I explained, and he said there was room. As it turned, out the plane was carrying fourteen full caskets and five body bags, each containing a dead American soldier. The stench from the decaying corpses in that sweltering heat and humidity was almost overpowering. That flight was the longest forty-five minutes of the entire war for me. My only response was to pray, both for the dead and their families — and to never forget.

I eventually adjusted to the heat. Living in Vietnam was like entering a country-sized sauna. You would bathe and dress in the morning and be

*Cambodia mission accomplished and ready to return to
R.V.N. (Republic of Vietnam), 29 June 1970*

soaking wet by the time you arrived for duty. One of the consequences of the heat, humidity, and uniforms was Jungle Rot. This was a fungus that caused rashes and infections. Most soldiers experienced this on their inner thighs. My own rash was manageable but it never entirely cleared up until I left Vietnam. But one of my officers experienced such a bad case that he had to go to the hospital where for several days he lay on his back, with his legs lifted off the sheets and spread to be exposed to sun lamps. This was the only effective way to kill the fungus that prevailed.

Aside from the fighting, the greatest threat to my health during my tour in Vietnam was the lack of sleep. We worked very long hours, usually sixty-to-seventy hour weeks. At one stage I worked seventy-two hours straight. One time I was so tired that I vomited continuously. I also came down with pneumonia twice. But all of us in the unit were fiercely committed to our mission and believed we could win the war. This was not some form of spying on Communist agents in a European city. It was the work of intelligence units in the midst of armed conflict. It seemed as if everything we did mattered because lives were on the line.

But we had times for relaxation and at the base in Saigon the best form of leisure was eating. I usually took my meals in the base cafeteria, though sometimes I ate at the officers club. The best meal I ate was at a little shack in a fishing village near Nha Trang. They served a crab chowder that was superb. But for simple pleasures, my favorite meal was the C-rations, especially the cans of peaches in syrup. I would take these back to my room and read letters from home and write them in return. Phebe was an incredible correspondent. She wrote every day. I didn't always receive her letters but the ones that did reach me were the highlight of my time away from conflict. The soldiers at the base played a lot of poker. We only bet nickels and dimes but over the course of an evening one could lose three dollars if your cards were bad. And, three dollars was the limit.

Even there, however, hostilities found a way to disturb the tranquility. One evening, as I was writing a letter to Phebe, I noticed movement out of the corner of my eye. I looked and saw a spider the size of a softball.

Rather than figure out how an exterminator would handle the problem I took the soldier's way out. I picked up my 38 and shot the big bug. Of course, my fellow officers knew what was going on. Killing a rat the size of a cat was also not unusual.

My time in Vietnam was challenging and rewarding. We could see progress. I also recognized the many problems facing us.

CHAPTER 55

Vietnamese

Eddie Adams' Pulitzer Prize-winning photograph of General Nguyen Ngoc Loan executing Nguyen Van Lém, a Viet Cong officer, was just one of many images that journalists sent back to the United States that raised doubts about the American presence in Southeast Asia. The image shows one man shooting another at point blank range — only separated by the length of the General's arm. It is set on a sunny day on one of the streets of Saigon, with a clear boulevard extending for several blocks. In the background, about six feet from the General, is a United States soldier, who appears to be holding up his arm to people beyond the frame of the photograph. This suggests that the United States military was implicated in an almost gangster-land style killing, in broad daylight, in a civic space for all the public to see. We were apparently holding people back so this General could kill this Viet Cong.

What was left out in the distribution of that photograph was the back story of what had happened the day before. Van Lém had been part of a death squad that assassinated thirty-four members of the South Vietnamese National Police and their families, including Ngoc Loan's children. Loan was later shot in Vietnam and seriously wounded, leading to the amputation of one of his legs. He later immigrated to the United States and opened a pizza restaurant in the suburbs of Washington, D.C. But once the public discovered his identity, as the killer in the

photograph, he was forced to retire. Some patrons even left threatening messages on the walls of the restaurant's bathroom.

What Ngoc Loan did was unfortunate but his retaliation for the loss of friends and especially the lives of so many family members who were not involved in the war is also understandable. Since boyhood I had seen this kind of brutality in the name of some political cause. Vietnam was no different, though for the most part the United States soldiers with whom I worked and for whom I had responsibility treated the enemy well (even the North Vietnamese prisoners). In fact, going back to my days in Italy, I always observed American soldiers as the most decent and honorable of the world's armies. United States military personnel would sometimes violate the Geneva Conventions governing warfare, but it was rare. Most of the time the reason for such action — as in the case of Ngoc Loan — was a reaction to an even greater enormity. Soldiers are human beings and the South Vietnamese were particularly vulnerable since they had their own families, homes, and towns to lose. If they behaved in ways that disgusted network news audiences, they usually did so for reasons that journalists too often neglected or distorted.

My own interaction with North Vietnamese prisoners was basically respectful. I still have a swagger stick hanging in my library, finely carved from walnut and capped with a steel point that prisoners made for me. When we captured them, our custom was to salute the officers and to treat them in a way that we ourselves would have expected as members of a class of fighters who tried to play by the rules of warfare. In some ways, my model for treating them was the one I had learned during my first tour of duty in Frankfurt — if you give them a better story than the Communist narrative, they will gladly abandon Communism. Of course, the real complication to this approach was the case of the guerilla soldiers. We had no solution for it then, and the United States' ongoing struggle with terrorism after 9/11 suggests that still no perfect solution exists to the problem of insurgents who target and attack civilians.

In many cases, the prisoners had no choice but to return to the Communist side. After we had held the prisoners for the allotted time — anywhere between two days and two weeks — we turned most of them over to a pacification program which would then train them to be integrated into the South Vietnamese army. The most recalcitrant of prisoners we would send to Phu Quoc, the penal island. But these soldiers were the ones who carved the swagger stick for me. We were under regular surveillance by Red Cross staff to insure the humane treatment of prisoners. The U.S. treatment of prisoners was in direct contrast to the experiences of U.S. military in the North Vietnam's prisons. Many of the enemy soldiers were poor farmers who eked out a subsistence existence. Unfortunately, the North Vietnamese would not permit farmers to return to their homes. Instead, they retrained the former prisoners and sent them back to the front lines. It seemed at times that the North Vietnamese, whose Communist ideology spoke well about the common man and women, viewed those ordinary folk as fodder to be used in a war of attrition until the United States grew weary or lost its nerve. It was arguably a good strategy, but did not say much about Communism and its treatment of its citizens.

The poor farmers were not the only ones to suffer during the war, though they bore the brunt of injuries and death. Vietnamese children also suffered. One of the most rewarding parts of my time in Vietnam was to help with and support orphanages run by Buddhist nuns just outside Saigon. I was involved directly with two of the existing orphanages and assisted in establishing a third. The United States military in informal ways encouraged American soldiers to give whatever they could to the orphans. We had no formal mechanisms for assistance, and in many cases would simply ignore policies that restricted the use of rations or medical supplies to our own soldiers. To see the children eat the food we brought from our own provisions made me happy. It also reminded me of the generosity I had received in Milano from American and British soldiers who took pity on a very skinny teenager.

Mike delivering food & clothing to one of the orphanages in Nha Trang, South Vietnam

The children had a lot of needs. One was hygiene. They lacked soap and once I let Phebe know, she was industrious in rallying the people at her church back in Syracuse to send packages of the soap, along with clothing and shoes. Shoes were especially important because the children ran around in flimsy sandals that did not prevent cuts and thus exposed them to bacteria. Their sores and infections were painful to see. At one point, I was able to have the military's surgeons visit and treat as many children's feet as they could. We repeated this exercise periodically.

The good-hearted nature of the United States soldiers also prompted many to assist in a variety of ways, even as simple as playing with the kids. It was therapeutic for soldiers who would be killing the enemy one day to be helping out some of the most needy Vietnamese the next. And from the military's perspective it was also an important form of community relations that we should have expanded dramatically.

After seeing the Montagnard people or the Vietnamese farmers conscripted into the military, it was hard not to think that this was a war that many people in the country did not want or need or know anything about. They were simply the residents of a place that rulers and officers in faraway places had determined to be of strategic importance in the conflict between the Communist East and the free West. Had the Vietnamese been able to sort out their affairs without the involvement of Americans, French, Chinese, or Russians, they would likely have as many difficulties as all peoples have had. My homeland of the Balkans is testimony to the difficulty of peoples with long histories and even longer memories living together peacefully. But it was also hard to conceive of this war, as important as it would have been in stopping the spread of Communism, was of much help to the ordinary Vietnamese.

One of the army officers assigned to Mike

CHAPTER 56

Seeing Results

Some say that the United States may have been conflicted during the Vietnam War, but the work of my unit rarely was. I understood that the United States' involvement in Vietnam was debatable. It was important to me to see Communism defeated wherever it appeared. I had seen how destructive it was in Europe during my childhood and I knew from intelligence work in Germany how tyrannical the Soviets were. But whether or not Vietnam was crucial to United States' interests was a different matter from the plight of the South Vietnamese. My main frustration with the Johnson administration (and some with Nixon's), as well as some military leadership provided by General William Westmoreland, was a lack of resolve to win the war. Too much of the Vietnam War played out in the media, and much of the reporting was anti-war. Too much of the war's strategy was viewed from the perspective of popular support rather than from realistic assessments of the conflict on the ground in Vietnam. But if we were going to go to war in the first place, we needed to commit to winning it. As determined as the North Vietnamese and Viet Cong were, and as unusual as the circumstances were (compared to World War II), I knew that the United States was winning the war and could have prevailed had the Johnson administration decided to go all out and had the press been objective. Let me give you one example.

Within my own sphere of operations, I experienced great satisfaction on many occasions with my unit's ability to acquire important intelligence that was crucial to the war's success. In one instance, my people in Cu Chi discovered the tunnels that the Viet Cong used in South Vietnamese towns to escape detection. The tunnels of Cu Chi were an immense network of connecting underground tunnels. Such tunnels actually existed throughout the country. These underground paths were in fact the Viet Cong's base of operations for the Tet Offensive. They functioned as hiding spots for Viet Cong guerrillas during combat, as well as serving as communication and supply routes, hospitals, food and weapon caches and living quarters for numerous guerrilla fighters. The system of underground fortresses were of great importance to the Viet Cong and gave them a real advantage in withstanding United States' technological superiority. I am convinced that the Air Force intelligence officers were the first to detect these tunnels, but did not immediately recognize their strategic significance.

Some in the United States military's leadership did not believe our reports at first, nor were they ultimately convinced of the need to dismantle the tunnels. Soldiers on the ground saw firsthand where the tunnels were and responded with ad hoc tactics, throwing grenades and engaging in some hand-to-hand combat. But the Cu Chi tunnels did not receive the sustained attention that they should have. Part of the problem was the danger involved in going through the tunnels. They were infested with insects, some of them poisonous, and were breeding grounds for illnesses, especially malaria, which was the second largest killer of the Viet Cong after armed combat. Our response to the tunnels was unsuccessful. When troops found a tunnel, they would often underestimate its size. Plus, the tunnels were rigged with explosive booby traps. The two standard ways of dealing with a tunnel opening were to flush the entrance with water to force the guerrillas into the open — using tear gas was against the Geneva Conventions — toss a few grenades down the hole and "crimp" off the opening. Because the tunnels used a fairly sophisticated system of trap doors and air filtration, our efforts were not very successful. Finally, the military trained units of "tunnel rats," specialists specifically responsible for going through the tunnels to gut them of their effectiveness. But this failed too since after these soldiers carried out their duties, the Viet Cong would return. Finally, in 1969 American forces resorted to carpet bombing the Cu Chi Triangle in hopes of knocking out the tunnels. By that point in the war it was too little, too late.

One of the most important pieces of intelligence in which I was also directly involved during the war was to trace the source of supplies to the North Vietnamese from outside the country. Most of us in the intelligence business suspected that armaments were coming through Cambodia and then transported to eastern Cambodian provinces on the border of South Vietnam. Satellite images, then a form of intelligence gathering in its infancy, confirmed this supposition. (Satellites were so novel at the time that we could not even use "satellite" in communications. We had to use code language.) We needed hard proof of what was on the ships going through the Cambodian ports of Sihanoukville. We knew that Bulgarian ships were going in and out of the port. They were supposedly carrying rice, as if the people in southeastern Asia needed rice from Eastern Europe.

I worked with one of the agents I had inherited from the previous unit commander because of my experience. He was a very effective spy and had a good network of associates. His first success was to acquire photographs of the ships' manifests — the documents describing the cargo on board. Those lists showed that the Bulgarians were shipping rice. But his next great coup was to produce photographs of the ships' cargo — to show what was inside those crates and boxes. Here we learned that the Bulgarians were shipping Soviet tanks, jeeps, weapons, and ammunition. Pressure came from the highest levels in Washington to confirm and monitor future shipments. It was the proof that the United States finally needed to show not only that Cambodia was a hostile government in the Vietnam War but also that the Soviets were aiding and abetting the North Vietnamese.

I went to Singapore and other places to meet an agent. I brought his payment in U.S. dollars. He brought the evidence. We met at a flophouse. I figured that going to the five-star hotels where so many of the intelligence personnel and business people transacted their business was a give-away of our efforts. This man gave me both photographs and microfilm. I was a little upset with him for bringing photos because they could easily be used to associate him with espionage and it would have been the end for him. But seeing the photos of the ship's manifest easily overcame my annoyance. I was elated, so much so that I decided to underscore the success in the way I paid him. When he went to use the bathroom, I laid out the U.S. currency covering the bed with small stacks of $100 bills. When he came out and saw the money his reaction was almost as joyous as mine in seeing the smoking gun of those photographs. This was a real coup.

This piece of intelligence contributed President Nixon's decision, at the advice of Henry Kissinger, to widen the war into Cambodia and Laos. The bombing raids that ensued in 1969 on North Vietnamese bases in Cambodia were exceptionally successful, but unfortunately, Defense Secretary Melvin Laird ordered all bombing in Cambodia to cease. Unfortunately, these raids also killed some civilians since the North Vietnamese often situated their military targets within neighborhoods and towns precisely to add a civilian buffer between them and American forces. Engagement with Cambodia also significantly destabilized the government. Ironically it set into motion changes within Cambodia that would lead first to the rule of the pro-United States General, Lon Nol, and then to the horrific and genocidal maniacal regime of Pol Pot and the Khmer Rouge (Communist).

The war in Vietnam was complex and brutal, and involved the United States in a region where it had very little history or understanding. But again, the lack of knowledge and a clear strategy for winning the war and securing a friendly and strong government able to resist Communist advances were reasons for not going to Vietnam in the first place.

General H.P. Smith awarding Mike
The Meritorious Service Medal —

Second Meritorious Service Medal —
for specific mission

CHAPTER 57

R&R

Intelligence on the movement of armaments from Bulgaria through Cambodia to the North Vietnamese was big news and pivotal for United States' involvement in southeast Asia. Information of this magnitude demanded more than simply passing along the photographs to officials in Washington or writing reports to be sent up the chain of command. It also demanded personal contact. The intelligence and foreign policy community in Washington wanted a complete set of data to fill in the obvious evidence taken by a friendly source. So when word came down that the Pentagon wanted an officer to brief military and civilian authorities about the situation in Cambodia, I immediately volunteered for the assignment. I had lots of experience writing detailed reports that were valued within the Pentagon, and other various federal agencies. I boarded a plane that took me first to Hawaii and then to the Bolling Air Force base just outside the nation's capital. I spent almost four days in Washington reporting to the different branches of the military and to the Departments of Defense, State, and National Security.

On the trip to Washington, I took four days of my annual leave to spend with Phebe and our children who were living in Syracuse, NY. What a gift to spend time with our daughter, Phebe, and our son, Mike, both of whom were growing up quickly and missed my presence, but not as much as I missed them.

Because I was in intelligence I could travel in civilian clothes much of the time. I witnessed no hostility for my involvement in the Vietnam War. But that was not the case for Phebe.

Phebe was not naïve about the situation. For this reason, she would not join the soldiers' wives' groups. She did not want our kids to experience any difficulty because of my tour of duty. She simply wanted to go about her business of rearing our children, volunteering at the schools and the church, and being a companion to her father, who by then had retired as a Methodist minister and superintendent.

Cover of the Foreign Policy Research Institute 2014 Annual Report.
Mike & Phebe were among the presenting sponsors at the dinner.

CHAPTER 58

Top Secret

As a career intelligence officer, I was involved in several highly classified operations that I still am unable to divulge. However, my work was recognized with the following two Presidential Citations — the Meritorious Service Medal and the Bronze Star, for my intelligence work in Vietnam and Cambodia.

I have also received a total of 16 various U.S. Military Medals and one South Vietnam Medal of Honor awarded during a parade in Saigon.

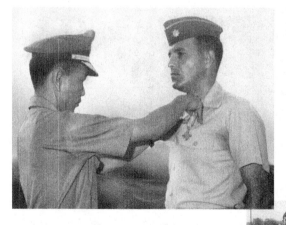

Mike receiving the
Vietnamese Medal of Honor
from
Vietnam Air Force Commander,
10 July 1970,
Saigon, South Vietnam

THE UNITED STATES OF AMERICA

TO ALL WHO SHALL SEE THESE PRESENTS, GREETING:

THIS IS TO CERTIFY THAT
THE PRESIDENT OF THE UNITED STATES OF AMERICA
AUTHORIZED BY EXECUTIVE ORDER, 16 JANUARY 1969
HAS AWARDED

THE MERITORIOUS SERVICE MEDAL
(FIRST OAK LEAF CLUSTER)
TO

LIEUTENANT COLONEL MICHAEL NOVAKOVIC

FOR

OUTSTANDING SERVICE
2 JULY 1976 TO 30 NOVEMBER 1978

GIVEN UNDER MY HAND IN THE CITY OF WASHINGTON
THIS 6th DAY OF FEBRUARY 19 79

CHIEF OF STAFF   SECRETARY OF THE AIR FORCE

AF FORM 2259, JUL 70

CITATION TO ACCOMPANY THE AWARD OF

THE MERITORIOUS SERVICE MEDAL
(FIRST OAK LEAF CLUSTER)

TO

MICHAEL NOVAKOVIC

Lieutenant Colonel Michael Novakovic distinguished himself in the
performance of outstanding service to the United States while
assigned to the Defense Intelligence Agency, from 2 July 1976 to
30 November 1978. As Chief, Soviet/Warsaw Pact Air Forces Branch,
Colonel Novakovic inspired a nearly five-fold increase in the production of finished intelligence documents relating to Soviet air
assets. This increased output, together with significant qualita-
tive improvement, greatly expanded the usability and worth of Air
Branch products to consumers worldwide. The singularly distinc-
tive accomplishments of Colonel Novakovic culminate a distinguished
career in the service of his country and reflect great credit upon
himself and the United States Air Force.

THE UNITED STATES OF AMERICA

TO ALL WHO SHALL SEE THESE PRESENTS, GREETING:

THIS IS TO CERTIFY THAT
THE PRESIDENT OF THE UNITED STATES OF AMERICA
AUTHORIZED BY EXECUTIVE ORDER, AUGUST 24, 1962
HAS AWARDED

THE BRONZE STAR MEDAL

TO

MAJOR MICHAEL NOVAKOVIC

FOR
MERITORIOUS SERVICE

4 August 1969 to 2 August 1970

GIVEN UNDER MY HAND IN THE CITY OF WASHINGTON
THIS   16th   DAY OF   June   19 70

GEORGE S. BROWN, General, USAF
Commander, Seventh Air Force

SECRETARY OF THE AIR FORCE

CITATION TO ACCOMPANY THE AWARD OF

THE BRONZE STAR MEDAL

TO

MICHAEL NOVAKOVIC

Major Michael Novakovic distinguished himself by meritorious service as Chief,
Military Exploitation Section, Detachment 6, 6499th Special Activities Group,
in the Republic of Vietnam, while engaged in ground operations against an op-
posing armed force from 4 August 1969 to 2 August 1970. During this period
Major Novakovic's outstanding professional skill and initiative in managing all
the United States Air Force's human intelligence collection teams in this theater, greatly contributed to the success of the intelligence collection capabilities of Detachment 6, 6499th Special Activities Group and the United States
Air Force in Southeast Asia. Major Novakovic's ability in directing this collection effort provided invaluable intelligence of theater as well as national
level interest and immeasurably contributed to the United States/Republic of
Vietnam combat effectiveness in the Republic of Vietnam and Cambodia. The ex-
emplary leadership, personal endeavor, and devotion to duty displayed by Major
Novakovic in this responsible position reflect great credit upon himself and
the United States Air Force.

CHAPTER 59

The End of an Era

When I left Vietnam in 1970, the long hours and war conditions had taken their toll on me physically. I was almost forty years old, certainly not an old man but by no means young. I had thrown myself into the work and believed — and still believe — we were winning the war and would have been successful if we had committed the resources and if the United States government had generated popular support back home.

I had other reasons for leaving Vietnam. My daughter and son were approaching adolescence when a father at home is especially important. I missed Phebe and the children. In Vietnam I realized that one of the great advantages of my previous assignments was that I could be with my family often while engaged in military intelligence. So an assignment back in the United States had great appeal at this stage of life.

From the vantage point of time in Vietnam I had already sensed a weakening of American resolve in the fight against Communism. Americans may have grown tired of their nation's position in maintaining a peaceful and stable political order in the face of Soviet expansionism, though the majority of United States citizens were far more supportive of the war and the nation's foreign policy than the students and faculty and other anti-war groups who attracted media coverage. Unfortunately, the media distorted the truth. But I was still very much cognizant of the role that the United States had played in reestablishing political order in Europe and the opportunities the nation afforded for a life free from the ideologies of socialism, nationalism, and fascism to immigrants like me. Not only was I grateful to the United States for saving my family's and my life and providing a secure and peaceful place to call home, but I knew through my own intelligence activities that Soviet Communism was not a matter that officials in Washington, D.C. or the Pentagon could ignore.

I also left Vietnam because I knew that the long-term prospects for victory were in decline. By 1970 Nixon's policy of Vietnamization was

one year old. This involved extracting United States forces from Vietnam and handing over the defense of South Vietnam to the Army of the Republic of Vietnam. The president urged "peace with honor,"

Military Outpost near Pleiku, South Vietnam

and employed means to demonstrate a strong United States. This posture included bombing Cambodia and Laos. The decision to hand over South Vietnam's defense to the Vietnamese allowed the United States to withdraw troops and to reposition combatants within the country away from the borders where casualties were heavy and into the interior and coastal regions.

I respected the South Vietnamese and when they awarded me their Honor Medal during a military parade in Saigon, I took comfort from the accomplishment. But I also knew that with the threat of the Democratic controlled Congress cutting off aid to the South Vietnamese, our allies were facing impossible odds against the North Vietnamese who continued to enjoy resources and support from China and the Soviet

Union. I was shocked that Nixon thawed relations with China. I saw the handwriting on the wall.

So I came back to the U.S to work in Washington. Phebe and I found a home in Alexandria, Virginia and I was assigned to Fort Belvoir, Virginia, where I worked on a classified project.

As a senior Major and an intelligence officer in the middle of his career, with some thought still of becoming a General, I was hardly close to retirement. After a time, I went to work in the Pentagon within the Air Force Plans office. Here my chief accomplishment was to develop the intelligence doctrine for the Air Force. I was part of the initial efforts by the United States military to build on its experience in twentieth-century wars and codify the best ways to conduct war according to the demands and technological realities of the twentieth century. I spent several months doing research at the Air University on Maxwell-Gunter Air Force Base in Mobile, Alabama. I read books on war from the ancient Chinese and nineteenth-century Prussians, works that I had never encountered at Syracuse University. My study was published. It became the basis of the first Air Force intelligence doctrine that contributed to the United States Air Force's eventual comprehensive statements that appeared in the 1990s.

After working on the intelligence doctrine, I was transferred to the Defense Intelligence Agency. Here I worked in the Command Post for all military intelligence. All the branches of the military provided staff for the unit where I worked and our reports circulated widely in the nation's capital — to the White House, Major Military Commands, the State Department (including all their world-wide facilities), National Security Agency, the CIA, and the FBI. We monitored reports from all over the world, wherever we had military intelligence officers, people doing work like I had done from Frankfurt and Wiesbaden. It was not nearly as grueling a pace as in Vietnam, but the work involved shifts of twelve hours a day, four days in a row, followed by three days off.

The reports we received in the alert center were prioritized according to their sensitivity and need for immediate response. During my time there in 1974 none of the information we processed required the Pentagon to deploy troops, ships, or aircraft. We learned of Soviet movements in different parts of the world and still monitored developments that were pertinent to the war in Vietnam. The defection of Lieutenant Viktor Belenko, a Soviet pilot who on September 6, 1976 successfully flew his Mikoyan-Gurevich MiG-25 jet fighter out of the Soviet Union to Hakodate, Japan, illustrates the kind of intelligence we received at the alert center. Belenko's act gave the United States and its allies unprecedented access to the capacities of this important Soviet aircraft. His account of the incident was published in his 1980 book: *MiG Pilot: The Final Escape of Lt. Belenko*. The Soviets insisted that the plane be returned. The West eventually gave the MiG back, but not until it was thoroughly examined, documenting its most sophisticated pieces of technology, better than any in our inventory.

Soon after I established a routine at the Pentagon, Major General H(arold). P. Smith requested I accompany him to San Antonio, Texas as his special operational assistant at the United States Air Force Security Services headquarters. Smith had served in World War II as a navigation instructor and a member of several crews based in the United States. After the war, he held a variety of posts before I met him at the Pentagon and came to know him as one of my favorite commanders. The chance to report to Smith offset the challenge that a move to Texas would bring to the family.

Since our marriage in 1956, Phebe and I had lived in Frankfurt, Germany; Milano, Italy; Vacaville, California; Carlisle, Pennsylvania; Springfield, Massachusetts; Denver, Colorado; Camp King, Germany; Wiesbaden, Germany, and now Alexandria, Virginia — all of this within fifteen years, not counting times like my year in Vietnam when we lived apart. My peripatetic ways as a boy were following me as an officer in the greatest country in the world. To Phebe's resumé as an elementary school teacher, she added San Antonio, Texas.

The United States Air Force Security Services were located at the Kelly Air Force Base in San Antonio, the oldest, continuously active air base in the United States. The base dated back to the United States' entry into World War I. It expanded operations to support American involvement in World War II, the Korean War, and the Vietnam War. The civilian leaders of San Antonio recognized the value of military operations for local development. Like so many cities in the United States with bases nearby, San Antonia was a "military town" that encouraged tremendous goodwill from the residents for soldiers. I recall once trying to make a reservation at one of the better restaurants and being turned down. One of my colleagues asked me if I had included my rank when giving my name. I had not. So I called back and asked for a reservation for "Colonel Novakovic." All of a sudden a table at the desired time was available.

Kelly A.F.B. was the base of operations for a variety of functions until 1953 when the Air Force located its Security Services headquarters there. The United States Air Force Security Services (USAFSS) was a secretive and tight-knit branch of the Air Force with responsibility for monitoring, collecting and interpreting military voice and electronic signals. At the time, military intelligence employed over 20,000 military personnel involved in gathering information around the world. USAFSS had two major areas of operations. The first, ground based units, were scattered throughout the globe and collected information electronically from fixed sites. The second, airborne units, flew from bases around the world, skirting sensitive areas and collecting data in a variety of aircraft.

As the special operational assistant to General Smith, most of the time I accompanied him to Washington, D.C. when he reported to the National Security Agency. But I also went out on my own as a senior officer to offer instruction in difficult circumstances that often arose. On one of my trips to Point Barrow, Alaska, the furthermost point of the United States, where the Air Force had a radar station just across the Bering Strait from Russia, I experienced an adventurous flight home.

After inspecting the station and interacting with the personnel, we boarded our plane to return to San Antonio. Less than midpoint on our flight we actually lost the use of three of the plane's four engines. It felt like we hit a wall. At this point, we were still twenty minutes away from the airport in Juneau. It did not look good. So we prepared to throw all non-essential baggage and material and jettisoned much of the food to take the strain off the lone working engine. After an emergency landing at Juneau, everyone on the flight was fine and no worse for the wear. This aircraft was not supposed to fly on one engine, but it did, on borrowed time.

One of my additional duties was to fly in reconnaissance planes. I was sent to jump school for a week's training. Although unusual for an officer with my experience, this training prepared me to join the first reconnaissance flight that went up to resume surveillance of China and the Soviet Union. After flying to Japan, I left from Okinawa and witnessed the remarkable performance and dedication that those pilots and crews displayed. Their flights often lasted twenty hours or more in cramped quarters that afforded little space for sleeping or relaxation when not on duty. In addition, the crews needed to prepare for the flights two days in advance. On this flight I saw first-hand the technological marvel of refueling these immense aircraft at altitudes over 20,000 feet while flying at speeds over 400 miles per hour.

What impresses me now as I reflect back on all my missions was the trust that the United States and its military invested in me, an immigrant from Eastern Europe. I was privy to material of unusual sensitivity and was the last foreign-born officer with such access that I knew of.

In 1974 we moved to the northern Virginia town of Springfield so that I could work at the Defense Intelligence Agency (DIA), where my responsibilities in the Soviet Air and Missile Forces Analytical Division involved assessing of the Soviet nuclear arsenal. The DIA had to serve and coordinate intelligence gathering efforts by the Navy, Army, and Air Force, which could be a complicated process.

In 1974, Congress passed the Hughes-Ryan Act, which required the president to notify the appropriate overseeing bodies about any collection of intelligence beyond the normal range of information gathering about foreign affairs. Then came the creation of the Senate Select Committee on Intelligence in 1975, followed by the House Permanent Select Committee on Intelligence in 1977. The rules governing these committees indicated a bi-partisan effort to bring congressional oversight to the work of United States intelligence. These reforms had an effect on all aspects of intelligence. One of the most striking changes was that for the first time in American history, Congress became a consumer of intelligence. Prior to this, the information collected by all branches of intelligence, circulated to the various layers of the executive branch of the United States government. Now, the eyes and ears exposed to classified information were more numerous. Even more potentially consequential was the problem posed by officials, subject to the regular cycles of elections, receiving intelligence reports. Many officials beyond the president could possibly use knowledge acquired through civilian and military intelligence agencies for the sake of re-election.

The CIA was subjected to closer inspection from Congress, and the DIA was undergoing its own internal scrutiny during the 1970s. The Kennedy administration had called for the creation of the DIA in 1961 for the precise purpose of greater efficiency among the branches of the United States military. In consultation with the Joint Chiefs of Staff, Robert McNamara at the Department of Defense sought a coordinated agency for managing the collection, processing, analysis, and dissemination of military intelligence, rather than having the Army, Navy, and Air Force guarding their own information and deploying their own operations. Initially the DIA performed as desired during crises like the one in Cuba when the agency supplied reliable intelligence on the Soviets' establishment of surface-to-air missile sites just off the Florida coast. My unit reported the Soviet invasion of Czechoslovakia in 1968; however, the warning was initially ignored by senior politicians.

To increase the agency's effectiveness, the DIA underwent a reorganization during the early 1970s that improved performance. In Vietnam, the Middle East, and South Africa the agency supplied important intelligence for policy makers and military strategists. The most significant mission for the agency during the 1970s was evaluating the Soviet Union's strategic nuclear and conventional capabilities. In the 1970s, the Soviets achieved rough parity with United States in nuclear forces, but questions remained about the Soviets' exact capabilities and intentions. DIA's analysts assisted civilian and military leaders in understanding the scope of Soviet forces. They also successfully managed many of the collection and analysis tasks upon which the Anti-Ballistic Missile (ABM) and Strategic Arms Limitation Treaty (SALT) agreements depended.

I was in charge of the unit that assessed the Soviets' nuclear air and missile capability. Precision was essential. If we overestimated the Soviets, then the United States would need to spend more on defense and retaliatory options than was necessary. Given the troubled economy of the 1970s, politicians, particularly the Democratic Party, were seeking measures to restrain military spending. At the same time, if we underestimated the Soviets' strength, we could make the United States vulnerable to a nuclear attack. No one in the military or Department of Defense wanted a devastating assault upon the nation on their watch. It was a fine line we needed to walk in assessing the Soviets' armaments.

Unlike my previous work, which had been in the field, I was now part of the military establishment inside the nation's capital at a time when intelligence was increasingly politicized. From one side came pressure to report on classified information during congressional hearings before people who, actually, were not qualified to know such intelligence. Granted, having to clear the room of congressional staffers several times for information restricted to congressional committee members only could make for a long and arduous meeting. But I became increasingly uncomfortable with the laxity I witnessed on Capitol Hill owing to new rules for supervising United States intelligence. It seemed to me that

America's politicians were losing heart in their resolve to fight Communism as much as they were trying to improve the nation's political structures.

From one side of the political persuasion, came pressure for us to report information that fit an administration's policy. For instance, the Carter administration had definite ideas about the size of the American military. President Carter also oversaw the disastrous — in my opinion — policy of reducing nuclear weapons in the negotiations leading up to the SALT II Treaty. To be sure, eliminating the threat of nuclear war was vital, but the president's aims, as many critics pointed out, were naïve, especially if the Soviet Union had actually gained parity with the United States. In this context, reports like the ones my colleagues and I were generating about the growth and increasing effectiveness of the Soviets' nuclear weapons were not well received by Carter administration officials. During one briefing, I heard directly from one White House official that I needed to bring my team's assessments more into line with the President's goals. My analysts and I studied at great length the intelligence on which the DIA position was base. To report otherwise would have been criminal and potentially devastating to our National Defense. I refused. I knew what the intelligence revealed. During my entire career, I never refused an order. But I knew the difference between an order and a suggestion. My obstinacy did not go unnoticed. I declined to testify in Congress. I later heard that because of my reports, I would never make General. That was very disappointing.

Nevertheless, my work in Washington involved duties that reminded me of the stakes involved in the fight against Communism. One of the most memorable of my non-technical assignments at the Pentagon was my role in 1978 as an escort officer on a team of United States military officials and security personnel that hosted a group of Yugoslavian Generals. During the 1960s and 1970s, Yugoslavia attempted to become a leader in the international non-aligned movement that would be independent from either Soviet or the West's dominance. This effort allowed the United States to woo Yugoslavia either to remain non-aligned or even develop closer ties to the West. The visit of the Yugoslavian military officials — about fifteen in all — was designed to show them a positive image of the United States. Since many of the Generals were Serbian, I was appointed as the leader of this mission. We traveled across the country in our own dedicated aircraft to show the Yugoslavs both the beauty of the United States, the sophistication of our armed forces, and the pleasantries of our society. After some seven days, we finished the trip in New York City. I returned to my old neighborhood to see the Bronx Bombers at Yankee Stadium. We had box seats for the game but I did not use those tickets. I wanted the Generals to sit in the bleachers and experience "regular" Americans. And that we did.

As enjoyable as that trip was, the time in New York City also brought back disquieting memories of my birthplace. We were instructed to keep the Generals away from churches to avoid sensitive or divisive subjects. But when we passed St. Patrick's Cathedral one day, one of the Generals stopped the group and asked to go in. As a good host I was not going to say no. So we entered the cathedral and walked through its gothic beauty. Later that night, as the Generals were drinking their nightcaps, the General who had asked to go into the cathedral was visibly upset. I asked what was wrong. He told me that his son, who was a staunch anti-Communist, had committed suicide because of his father's involvement with the Communist Party. It was a sobering and sad reminder of the destructive political ideologies that continued to fester in Eastern Europe. Note: I attempted to find him, but he passed away.

After a couple of years in the DIA, I decided to leave the military. I witnessed a level of distrust and insincerity that was not what I had seen twenty-five years earlier in the United States and its military. This was a problem not simply among civilians in the federal agencies or the military officials who reported to the civilians. It was also part of the way that the nation's capital worked. In 1978, I had an option to take a plum assignment in Europe as a special operational assistant to a three-star General responsible for the entire European and African intelligence operations on the continent. As tempting as this was for the possibility of becoming a General (maybe the Carter official would forget his threat), our daughter was about to enroll at Smith College. Phebe and I also worried that if I stayed in for one more tour, I would have trouble establishing myself in a civilian career. We had seen several colleagues remain in the military one assignment too many and then need several years to find a suitable job.

So on August 15, 1978, I retired from a way of life that I had known for almost a quarter of a century. I did so with regret. I had loved the intelligence work and the United States military and was proud of my accomplishments. Chances are that if I had stayed in and received one more promotion, I would have experienced even more new efforts to supervise American intelligence. I left the military for the uncharted waters of life as an American civilian.

Mike swearing in Mike, Jr. at U.S. Air Force Academy, Colorado Springs

Part Four

From an Officer
to a Businessman

CHAPTER 60

Once an Entrepreneur, Always an Entrepreneur

I had not labored outside the military since law school when I worked briefly for an insurance company in Pennsylvania. With one child enrolled at an elite liberal arts college and another on his way to college (it turned out our son, Mike, wanted to go to the Air Force Academy), I did not have the luxury of choosing my ideal career. I had doubts that many companies would be interested in a middle-aged retired intelligence officer. It helped that Phebe had a career of elementary school teaching behind her. Her salary would certainly keep us afloat. But my options were not obvious. For that reason, I enrolled at a course at Catholic University of America designed for officers making the transition from military to civilian life. It was thorough, from offering advice on attire for interviews, to giving tips to wives who would also be interviewed informally at meals or social functions that were generally part of a round of interviews.

After one executive position in which I differed with the company's president, I decided to start my own company. It may have been twenty-five years since I was an entrepreneur as an undergraduate at Syracuse University, but I was still a hard worker and knew how to be successful as a businessman. The first question was what business. The second was how to finance it.

My knowledge of the Reagan administration's plans to cut military spending proved important. Part of the way to do this was to minimize the amount of maintenance needed to keep the ships running. Some of this maintenance was obvious — preventing rust — which included constant swabbing of the decks to sanding and painting all of the ships' surfaces while in dry docks spread out around the country. I decided to create a high-grade paint that could outlast other varieties and so reduce costs and manpower. Our name was Metallic Ceramic Coatings, Inc. And through trial and error in makeshift "laboratories," originally in Bridgeport, Pennsylvania (about twenty-five miles northwest of Philadelphia), my chemists and I concocted a unique paint mixture that included silver powders. In the early years, when we were getting by on a shoe-string, I was mixing some of the materials in kitchen blenders. But the formulas worked, and when the company eventually became popular, the silver additives gave us a leg up against competitors. How many could claim that customers' metallic parts would be coated in silver?

The more difficult question was how to finance this enterprise. Despite a small salary for much of my career, Phebe and I had managed to save a nice nest egg. We also had some profits from the sale of each of our homes in northern Virginia during my two stints with DIA. But this was hardly enough for the equipment and materials needed to make the company profitable. In addition to the ingredients that went into our coatings, and the machines to mix the paint, the company needed ovens — some 50 feet long and 15 feet wide. Early on, a huge help came from a German-American businessman from the Frankfurt section of Philadelphia, whose industrial facility after 30 years went out of business. He was willing to sell me his ovens and other equipment largely on the basis of a gentleman's agreement that I would pay him off in installments after my first six months of running the business. It took four months before I signed my first contract.

The early 1980s was a poor time to start a company in the United States. The cost of money was more expensive than at any time after

World War II. Between 1973 and 1982 the country's economy slid into a state of stagnation. The GNP reached a low of 1.8 percent for the final years of the Nixon presidency down to the first year of Reagan's administration. Unemployment rose as high as 8.3 percent during the mid-1970s, and the average rate of inflation for this decade was almost 9 percent. Adding to the economic woes of the nation was an energy crisis that sent the price of gas above levels Americans had ever seen, and forced them to wait in line for gas for unprecedented lengths of time. At one point in 1979, sixty percent of the nation's gas stations closed because of the shortage of fuel. Meanwhile, the prospects for borrowing money for businesses like mine were bleak. In response to high inflation, President Carter had already tasked the chairman of the Federal Reserve Board with contracting the money supply. This policy shot interest rates up to between 15 and 20 percent, and made business loans extremely expensive.

This economic environment did not deter me from my designs to own my own company, but it did mean I had to seek creative ways of financing the operation.

Mike as businessman — racing car sponsored by his company

When I first started my initial contracts with a large corporation, it generated about $5,000 of business per month. The product was so successful that within the first year, the company was doing $5,000 of business per week. The growth was entirely through civilian contracts. Private businesses and individuals often learned about us often by word of mouth and we coated everything from the muffler on a farmer's tractor to the chain link fence of oil companies on the Gulf Coast. But the real breakthrough for the company occurred after we found out about the market for coating race car parts. We did a little business with NASCAR but the main source of revenue came from the drag racing circuit. At this point, for advertising purposes we used the name, Jet-Hot Inc. Before our incredible success among drag racers, we were billing at a rate of over $10 million per year.

We also began to solicit more business among drag racers. (I also tried to generate customers in the NASCAR circuit.) The After Market Show was an annual drag racing convention in Las Vegas, Nevada that attracted roughly 150,000 participants. It became the time for Jet-Hot to pull out all the stops, send out our sales force, and "do" business. It was also a social time for the company. Staff members brought along their spouses who helped in marketing and took advantage of the resort's shows and restaurants. Phebe also came and oversaw the entire social calendar. She generally enjoyed the conventions but could never understand why you needed over 1,000 booths, each promoting a seemingly different and more advanced hubcap. Once, when a few of the sales staff were on a break, she even tried to sell our product at our booth. After talking for a few minutes, the crew manager said, "Lady, you don't know a damned thing about cars, but I am going to buy your product anyway."

I would also like to think that our success did not simply owe to the good fortune of free publicity. We offered a good product at a reasonable rate, charging $200 per production hour. This was higher than competitors but we argued, and eventually proved, that our coating lasted much longer and was cheaper in the long run. When we started to expand, one of the plant managers advised me that a month turnaround on the process would be reasonable. I thought that was far too slow. So we made it our policy to return pieces to customers, cleaned and coated, within five days. Over time we reduced this to forty-eight hours. In addition to offering a superior product, we were fast. And I tried to instill an ethos of service and quality at all levels of the company. The line that "the customer is always right" has become a cliché, but it was an important part of my company's success. Our customers' trust in us was remarkable since many of the parts were irreplaceable.

To keep up with the growing business we started facilities in places outside Philadelphia, where at the peak of our operations we employed over ninety people and were doing many million dollars worth of business a year. We established those plants in Pascagoula, Mississippi, and Phoenix, Arizona. These plants gave us access to regions where car racing was strong but also coverage across the nation to maintain a quick return on orders. Expansion looked like a godsend when several calamities struck our facilities in Pennsylvania. In 1999, Bridgeport, the site of our mixing and coating plants, as well as our business offices initially, experienced a flood on the Schuylkill River that was historic. The flood waters reached a record level and destroyed most of our equipment and all of our office's files and paperwork. We had no flood insurance because the river had no record of cresting this high. To get by, we needed to do some fast and fancy financing.

A few years later, our reopened plants along the Schuylkill River were destroyed once again, this time by a fire that devastated the entire complex of industrial buildings of which we were part. Ironically, this catastrophe had the silver lining of insurance refunds allowing us to buy new equipment that made the company much more efficient. At that time we placed the manufacturing component of our business in Quakertown, Pennsylvania and our offices in King of Prussia, Pennsylvania.

But the worst of all the disasters was Hurricane Katrina which completely destroyed our Mississippi plant and many of our workers' homes. When the storm hit, I was calling my managers constantly because I could see that the storm could cause real problems for the Pascagoula facility. I had bought them cell phones so that I could contact them whenever I needed. But they weren't answering my calls. Their phones were now dead and my staff had no way to recharge their phone batteries. Finally, one of the managers called me. I asked what they needed most. He said cash because not even the cash machines were working. So I decided that I would fly to Mississippi and bring cash to tide employees over until they could resume work. (Little did I know how long it would take to reopen in Pascagoula.)

We learned all of this on a Saturday and the only way for us to withdraw sufficient amounts of cash was to contact our personal bank. They graciously opened the vault and we took as much as we could out of our savings. Our staff had warned us about vandalism in Mississippi, so I placed tens of thousands of dollars in a money belt that I wore underneath my clothing, an act that resembled the trip from Split to Trieste when I hid gold coins underneath my pants and shirt. When I arrived in Mississippi I could not believe the destruction. I distributed the money rapidly and my brother Paul, living in Florida, drove from his home with food. Because the Mississippi workers had no work or homes (for many of them), I divided them into three teams. One team worked on their homes, the second on renovating the factory and the third team went to Arizona. They would work for two weeks, and then rotate. This was good for the company because now most of the cleaning and coating was shifting to the Arizona plant where we needed more manpower. It was also good for the workers who needed places to live and pay checks to survive. Unfortunately, some of the Mississippi workers never returned to Pascagoula even after the plant reopened. The memories of Katrina were too strong and painful to endure. I tried to soften the pain by giving them generous severance packages.

Phebe provided invaluable assistance during those days. She contributed to Jet-Hot in other ways, especially helping to put the office work in better order (not one of my strong suits). For a while my daughter Phebe, who became an even more successful business executive than I, had also worked for me briefly. In general, I preferred to keep work and family separate, perhaps an attitude retained from working so long in a field where such a distinction was imperative. Ironically, Phebe may have seen more of me when I owned a company in the United States than when I was an intelligence officer.

As successful as Jet-Hot was — to the point of making us wealthy — it never seemed as important as my work in Intelligence. I was always more intent on defeating Communism than on making money. But with the hindsight of retirement I now understand better that by establishing a business, providing a worthwhile service, and employing staff in different parts of the country, and helping people, I was still fighting Communism. The strategy and weapons were different. But the results were not. By acting independently as a private citizen in the exchange of goods and services, I was helping to sustain a free society, and proving the superiority of the American system to the oppressive and collectivist strategies of the Communist system. I still marvel at the opportunities that the United States offered to me and my family, from providing a safe and secure place, to live to nurturing an economy that could allow an immigrant of modest abilities and lots of energy to make a fortune.

CHAPTER 61

What Made America Great

After I sold the company in 2007, Phebe and I traveled to Croatia. It was my first visit there since I left with my family in 1942 to sail to Pula. The cities of Split and Knin, along with the surrounding countryside, were beautiful. The trip also provided a few surprises. We were amazed by how beautiful and prosperous those cities appeared. But what was truly remarkable during this trip was learning that I was heir to properties and titles that my family possessed when I was a child. Part of the conditions for Croatia to be admitted into the European Union included returning the property confiscated by the Communist government to the rightful owners. The part of the Diocletian Palace where my maternal grandparents lived had now been returned to my family, with the deed being in my possession. This was the place where a good Sunday meal included finding a gold coin under my dinner plate. Incredible as it is to think that I now own a part of a Roman Emperor's retirement palace built over 1700 years ago on the Adriatic Sea, almost as difficult to fathom is that the Yugoslavian government actually preserved the papers that enabled the current officials to locate the original owners. The residence of my grandparents has now been divided into four flats — one on each level. Because of the proximity to the water and to the most high-end shopping district in Split, they would attract a high sum if, in consultation with the rest of my family, I put them up for sale. No matter their value, it is a rare citizen of the United States who owns a part of a palace built for the Roman Emperor Diocletian, who ruled from 284 – 305 A.D.

On this trip I was also surprised to hear that technically I could claim the title of Duke in the family in one of the Balkan territories. That is another rank that I could add to my titles of Colonel selectee and president of an American corporation. (Uncle Vlado was awarded the title of Duke thanks to his military services). When Phebe and I, on the same trip, visited the Novakovic hometown of Knin, Croatia, I spent time with the city's officials, several of whom informed me that I was next in line to inherit the lands that my Uncle Vlado had owned thanks to his military service in the Yugoslavian Royal Army. The property, most of which is undeveloped and uncultivated farm land, extends to 1,000's of acres. And if I were to become the legal holder of the title, the rank of Vojvoda (King's General — Duke) would also come to me. As I write, I am still unsure if I will take possession of the land, if only because I do not know if it will sustain a commercial enterprise profitable enough to pay the property taxes.

These ties to the old country were poignant and even amusing at some level but obviously did nothing to diminish my identification with and gratitude to the United States. For my siblings, my parents, and me, the Old World never had any appeal once the Communists and Fascists overturned our home and way of life. Aside from Gordana, who settled in Buenos Aires before the rest of the family immigrated to New York, all of the Novakovics became United States citizens and remain thankful for the life they have enjoyed. My father worked for several years first as a porter in a hotel and then as an accountant for Sheraton Hotels in New York before moving to Carlisle, Pennsylvania where he worked in the accounting department for a small oil company. When he retired, he and my mother lived for a while in Connecticut before relocating near my brother in Florida. My oldest sibling, Deana, worked for many years in New York City. She eventually married a successful business man from Connecticut who sadly died from cancer after five years of marriage. Deana took other jobs and retired to Florida. Gordana, the second oldest child, raised a family of four with her husband who owned one of the largest carpet making companies in South America. She suffered from a rare form of cancer and died prematurely in 1990. Paul, the youngest, served in the U.S. Navy as an officer for four years. As a civilian he first worked for a large U.S. corporation as the senior vice president of operations in South America, before starting his own company. Despite business ties to South America, Paul remained in the United States. For a family who arrived in New York City with only two gold coins (worth about $200) and even fewer contacts, we did well. Only in the U.S.A.

Of course, we started with very little. Even my mother, who had the hardest time giving up the life she knew in Split, expressed no regrets about living in the greatest nation on earth. That greatness was evident to us not only with the outcome of World War II, but also in the opportunities provided to immigrants like us to become citizens, establish homes, and even enjoy prosperity. When the subject of Communism came up, my mother spoke of joining the U.S. Army.

The superiority of the United States is especially evident in the way it enables immigrants, with no familiarity with American customs, to assimilate while also maintaining parts of their past identities. When fundraisers for the university contacted Phebe and me about giving help to construct a Meštrovic garden, we were glad to do so. A gifted sculptor whose works are now on display throughout the world, thanks to Syracuse University's project, the same is true for upstate New York where a half-dozen of Meštrovic's works are on display on the campus and at Notre Dame University in Indiana.

Another tie to my Serbian and Croatian past was religion. Phebe and I each maintained our affiliations with the churches of our childhoods and reared our children in each tradition, our daughter in the Methodist Church and our son in my own Eastern Orthodox communion. These distinctions were never hard and fast. I usually attend church with Phebe and our family often attended the Serbian Orthodox parish for high holy days.

I want to express some heartfelt sentiments about our country. Since I first started to write this book, our government has drifted to the very left, a move I find very disturbing.

Today, I urge our politicians from the President on down not to try to change our country. The foundation of our society is the Constitution and that has served us well. Certainly there are always ways to keep improving, but it was John F. Kennedy who proclaimed:

> *"Ask not what your country can do for you.*
> *Ask what you can do for your country."*

My wish is that we as a people follow these words because as a nation we have been a beacon to others. We are proud of our individual rights and our true democratic decision-making and have not taken the path of the failed doctrines of Socialism or Communism, although I observe a creeping temptation which must not afflict us.

If my life has any significance beyond my family, former military brothers, employees, and the nation I unhesitatingly served, it lies in the contrast between the Europe where I grew up, and the United States where I thrived as an adult. Without the United States intervention into World War II and the defeat of Hitler and Soviet Communism, it is hard to fathom how those pernicious ideologies would have been defeated. In addition to fighting some of the worst political regimes in human history, the United States also afforded a safe harbor for life, liberty, and the pursuit of happiness. My fear is that my fellow citizens are forgetting a historical era when the United States was truly a source of hope for most oppressed people in the world. I also worry that Americans are losing sight of the kind of society that values freedom, honor, responsibility, and industriousness. Perhaps, if others read about the life of an obscure boy from Split and his surprising journey to Villanova, Pennsylvania, they will marvel not at the boy or the man he became, but at the nation that made such a journey possible.

I remain eternally grateful to the United States of America.

God Bless the
United States of America,
Land of the Free.
Home of the Brave.